6/04

Coubertin's OLYMPICS

Coubertin's OLYMPICS

How the Games Began

DAVIDA KRISTY

LERNER PUBLICATIONS COMPANY
MINNEAPOLIS

For Kris: behind me with a pencil

Author Acknowledgments
Many people have made contributions to the accuracy and
completeness of this book. The author's gratitude goes to Wayne
Wilson, Ph.D., and Shirley Ito, M.L.S., of the Amateur Athletic
Foundation Library, to Gary Allison of the First Century Project,
and to Patricia R. Olkiewicz of the library staff at the U.S. Olympic
Training Center in Colorado Springs, Colorado. She also thanks
M. Geoffroy de Navacelle of Mirville, France, Joanne Burch, Terry
Dunahoo, Joan Prestine, Ann Alper, Karen Eustis, Herma Silverstein,
Dawn Miller, and Larry Zwier.

This book is available in two editions:
Library binding by Lerner Publications Company
Soft cover by First Avenue Editions
241 First Avenue North, Minneapolis, Minnesota 55401

Library of Congress Cataloging-in-Publication Data

Kristy, Davida.
    Coubertin's Olympics : how the games began / by Davida Kristy.
      p. cm.
    Includes bibliographical references and index.
    ISBN 0-8225-3327-8 (lib. bdg.)
    ISBN 0-8225-9713-6 (pbk.)
    1. Coubertin, Pierre de, 1863-1937—Juvenile literature.
    2. Sports promoters—France—Biography—Juvenile literature.
    3.Olympics—Revival, 1896—Juvenile literature. [1. Coubertin,
    Pierre de, 1863-1937. 2. Sports promoters. 3. Olympics.]
    I. Title.
    GV721.2.C68K75 1995
    338.4'7796'092—dc20
    [B]   94-12889

Manufactured in the United States of America
2 3 4 5 6 7 – JR – 01 00 99 98 97 96

Contents

Prologue

The noise from the streets built like thunder, coming closer and closer. People in the stadium seats strained to hear what the crowd outside was shouting.

This was the last event of a great athletic meet. And it was the first recorded competition in such a long race: a "marathon," more than 26 miles (40 kilometers) through the villages and countryside outside Athens. Crowds along the route cheered wildly as the runners passed.

As the shouts of the crowd rolled like a wave toward the seated audience, a man on horseback rode into the arena and up to the royal viewing box. He said something to the king and queen of Greece, and soon his thrilling news spread around the grandstand: "A Greek! A Greek is winning!" Joyfully, the chant was taken up by the crowd, which was largely Greek. One of their own countrymen had finally broken the string of American victories in this meet. In a few grueling hours, this Greek runner had restored the honor of his country.

Then the runner, Spiridon Loues, staggered through the entrance to the stadium. Elated spectators clambered from their seats and flooded onto the field to welcome him. They might have overwhelmed him, preventing him from reaching the finish line. But two of Greece's princes, George and Constantine, reached Loues first. Protecting him from the crowd, they jogged with him for the final lap around the field to the finish line.

Then the princes lifted him onto their shoulders and carried him to the royal box. The king waved his gold-encrusted hat so hard he tore the brim from the crown. Flowers rained on the runner. Women took off their jewelry and tossed it to him.

Spiridon Loues

The first Olympic marathon ended by creating a new Greek national hero. Athenians celebrated Loues's victory for days.

It was April 15, 1896. The first Olympic Games of modern times were over.

They had been simple games, with fewer than 30 events. Only 14 nations had competed. But the nine days of competition had been strenuous, exciting, and profitable. Those who participated, whether athlete, organizer, or spectator, could not help believing that the success of the Games would be repeated and that an international tradition had begun.

But, over the next hundred years, the Games would face many threats. War, politics, pettiness, and commercialism would each attack the fragile institution. Especially during the early years, the Games would struggle to maintain not only their identity but their very existence. That they preserved both is a credit to the industry of one French aristocrat who was barely noticed at the first modern Olympics.

And, after those first Games had ended—while Athens celebrated Greece's Olympic glory—the Frenchman, Baron Pierre de Coubertin, slipped quietly out of town. He had created these Games and brought them to life, but there were no shouts of praise for him.

Loues, after receiving his medal

Pierre de Coubertin as a young man

1

A Search for Strength

When Baron Pierre de Fredy de Coubertin (pronounced like koo-bear-TAN, but without a strong "N" sound) was a boy, no one bothered to ask what he would do when he grew up. He was a French aristocrat; most people assumed he would do what all wealthy nobles did.

Some aristocrats chose to live an elegant life with no real career. High-born people supported charities, dabbled in art or science for their own pleasure, took long vacations, and raised families to do the same things.

If a nobleman had energy and ambition, he could become a commanding officer in the French army, a priest, or a member of the government. But he probably would not be paid for such work. French aristocrats felt it was their privilege and responsibility to lead their country. Accepting pay would be dishonorable, like a wealthy person taking money from a very needy person. In any job, a member of the French nobility would work as an amateur—

Coubertin's Olympics

A self-portrait of Baron Charles-Louis de Coubertin

someone motivated by a love of the work, not by a desire to earn money. Similarly, an aristocrat who won an athletic contest would accept only a medal or a certificate, not a cash prize. This set the noble amateur apart from lower-class athletes—professionals who played for pay. If the young Baron Pierre de Coubertin didn't want to be a man of leisure, an officer, a priest, or a legislator, he would have to create a new style of life for himself.

Pierre was born in his parents' Paris apartment at 20 rue Oudinot (Oudinot Street) on New Year's Day, 1863. This apartment, which took the entire third floor of the five-story building, was filled with furniture from the finest woodworkers and decorated with works by well-known artists. Gold-trimmed books lined the library shelves, and one light and open room served as Pierre's father's atelier—his art studio, where he painted and taught others to paint.

Pierre's father, Baron Charles-Louis, was an artist of good reputation. His murals decorated many churches. As an aristocrat, he usually donated his fees to charity. He painted for the honor of his art. The family had plenty of money already.[1]

Detail from one of Charles-Louis's paintings. This piece depicts the re-establishment of the Olympic Games.

The subjects Pierre's father chose to paint came from myths, religious stories, and romantic poems. He also liked to illustrate incidents that glorified the history of France. He painted in strict accordance with artistic tradition, and his work was exhibited at salons—shows of France's great contemporary painters. These were the same shows that excluded the works of Paul Cézanne, Édouard Manet, and Pierre-Auguste Renoir, who have since eclipsed traditionalists like Charles-Louis de Coubertin.

Pierre's father may have used the traditional style because he liked it, but using it was also a political statement for him. It explained who he was: a man of the old order, who resisted upstarts and their revolutions. He hoped to see a king from the royal Bourbon family rule France once again.

Pierre's mother, Agathe, was born to a family with land in Normandy, a northwestern province of France. She inherited an estate in Mirville, and it was there that Pierre spent his early childhood and most of the summers of his youth.

Agathe made her Catholic religion into a career. She collected paintings of scenes from the Bible, as well as cups and plates used for serving Mass. She raised money for the church and did charity work among the farm families around Mirville.

Pierre had two older brothers and a younger sister. Baron Paul, the eldest, grew up to be a poet, but not a great one. Baron Albert became an army officer. Though Pierre was not the eldest son, the French system of nobility allowed all three Coubertin brothers to carry the title of baron and to share in the family fortune. Marie was raised, as were all French girls of her social class, to be charming and capable and to marry a man like her father and her brothers. She loved horseback riding, and she attended science lectures at a Paris university.

Part of Pierre's heritage was his family's motto: "See far, speak true, act firm." But Pierre was not very old before he realized that if he spoke what he thought was true, his father would be the one to act firm. It turned out, nevertheless, that Pierre could see far—much farther than his relatives.

A Search for Strength

Chateau de Mirville, where Pierre spent most of his summers

Though his brothers and sister were blonds, Pierre had thick, dark hair. He was not a truly handsome boy, but his looks improved as he grew older. Even in an age when few men grew to be six feet tall, Pierre was short. Fully grown he never measured more than five feet, three inches (160 centimeters) tall. Although he would never be big, it was important to Pierre to be strong.

According to the French way of thinking, a person earned honor by acting on his or her beliefs. Pierre believed he must do something to bring honor to himself and his family, and such deeds would require strength of character and body. Loss of honor because of lack of moral or physical strength would be deeply humiliating.

The entire French nation suffered this kind of hu-

miliation in 1871, when Pierre was only eight years old. In that year, France lost a war to Prussia, a part of what is now Germany. During this Franco-Prussian War, German troops besieged Paris, and the Coubertins fled to Mirville. When the siege was lifted, the German generals demanded high taxes and changed the government to suit themselves. The presence of these Germans reminded the French every day that their army had been too weak to win the war. The French people were ashamed, and, even at this early age, Pierre shared this feeling.

What was there about Germans, Pierre wondered, that made them better soldiers than the French? He asked a lot of questions, and one thing he learned was that many ordinary German men joined private groups that exercised together. The groups were called turnvereins, and the men who belonged called themselves "turners."

Turners did not play sports. Their goals were to make each man a good German citizen and a sturdy physical being. The group learned to synchronize their rhythmic movements until they moved as one. They didn't form teams or leagues, and they didn't compete. They just exercised. Wherever there was room for 10 or 20 men to work out, the turners met and ran their drills. They did stretches, bends, and jumping jacks; they swung heavy weights that looked like large bowling pins. When Germany needed an army, many men who joined were turners—already more fit than the average Frenchman.

German turners were part of a larger European trend toward fitness. In middle Europe (roughly the present-day Czech Republic and Slovakia), groups called sokols arose for the same purpose and with the same general routines as the turnvereins. Sokol and turner chapters were imported to the United States after people from middle Europe immigrated to America in the early 20th century.

Pierre gathered information about the turners, and about many other subjects, on his own. He studied with tutors, but his real education came from his trips through the city of Paris and from his hikes near the chateau in Mirville.

Opposite page, top: Pierre at age six. Opposite page, bottom: The Franco-Prussian War (1870-1871) led Pierre to explore the role of fitness in society.

Pierre got the kind of exercise any child gets. He climbed hills and trees, he swam, he ran and walked through the woods. He played rough games with his brothers and the children of Mirville. But he didn't know any adult French people who exercised like the turners.

When Pierre was 11 years old, he entered a Paris school run by Jesuit priests. It was called the Collège Saint-Ignace de la rue Madrid (Saint Ignatius School on Madrid Street). If he expected his schoolmates to exercise like turners with him, or to play sports or

German Turners

The founder of Turnerism, Frederick Ludwig Jahn, lived in a time when France, led by Napoleon, conquered part of Germany. Just as Pierre wondered why Germans were able to conquer France, Jahn wondered how the French could defeat Germany. He took it upon himself to educate a new generation of soldiers.

In 1811, Jahn opened a gymnasium in Berlin, where he taught children a particular system of exercise. He detailed this system in a book, *Nationality*, and teachers all over Germany began to use it as a text.

Jahn's system consisted of three elements:

1. Elective exercises, in which each turner could practice his favorites among such activities as running, vaulting, climbing ropes or poles, or even swimming.

2. Obligatory class gymnastics, which all participants did in unison, and which included marching and working with light apparatus.

3. Games, designed to foster alertness, judgment, and decision-making abilities.

Each session began and ended with a patriotic song. Often, these songs, and the sermonlike talks that followed, preached German unity and liberty. Liberty was not an idea that pleased the king of Prussia. So in 1819, Jahn found himself in jail, charged with demagoguery—stirring up people with false ideas to gain power. After waiting five years for a trial, he was found innocent. Even so, he was not allowed to teach turning.

Eventually, a new Prussian king decided to control turnerism, rather than suppress it. He brought back the old classes, and they regained their popularity.

Turnerism was brought to the United States by German immigrants. Turner societies continued in America until well after World War II, when local organized sports became far more popular.

organized games, Pierre had to be disappointed. The teacher-priests never exercised anything but their brains, and they expected the same from their students. There was no "recess"—no time to walk or run about. There was no gymnasium, no physical education class. Pierre spent 11 hours a day hunched over his desk, doing lessons in Greek and Latin, mathematics and history. His parents hoped the school's strict religious atmosphere would lead Pierre to a career in the priesthood.

As he entered his teens, Pierre's summer activities became more organized. He rode horses, and he took lessons in fencing, rowing, and boxing. Boxing practice was something to hide from his parents, who would have insisted that boxing was no sport for a gentleman.

Good at his studies, Pierre was one of the top three students in his class. He was distinguished by his ability to analyze concepts and ideas instead of just memorizing facts. For instance, by looking at the coins in his pocket, each with the profile of a different French leader stamped on its face, he understood that governments come and go. He also recognized that one could love a country and still see its faults.[2] None of these private thoughts would have pleased his parents, but he learned to be diplomatic, telling them only what would please them or phrasing his ideas in ways they could accept.

When he had free time, Pierre enjoyed reading. One of his favorite books was *Tom Brown's School Days,* an 1856 novel about life in an English boarding school. Tom Brown is a fictional character, but the story takes place at a real school, Rugby. At Tom Brown's Rugby, boys were encouraged to ask their teachers questions. Small boys (and Pierre was very small) often won fights with bigger ones. Boys could form clubs for almost any purpose. They played cricket, soccer, rugby-style football, and other competitive sports, which helped them to understand winning, losing, and cooperative effort.

From history class, Pierre knew the English had beaten the French and their general, Napoleon Bonaparte, at the Battle of Waterloo. He heard about

Pierre came to believe that bodies strengthened by sport... had made Englishmen into the kind of soldiers who could beat Napoleon's army.

a remark supposedly made by the Duke of Wellington, the English general who had engineered England's victory: "The Battle of Waterloo was won on the playing fields of Eton." Eton is another British school which, like Rugby, had a strong sports program. Pierre came to believe that bodies strengthened by sport, and courage, learned through competition, had made Englishmen into the kind of soldiers who could beat Napoleon's army.

Pierre's parents didn't admire England at all. They were ultra-conservative aristocrats who believed in restoring the French government to a king descended directly from Louis XVI. Any sign that one of their children should criticize French institutions like the schools or the church was met with horror. Pierre had many thoughts that set him apart from his parents, but he understood his mother and father and didn't want to offend them. He held to his personal ideals, but quietly, and did not openly rebel.

The Coubertin family did not treat rebels kindly. Pierre heard stories about a great-uncle who had joined a progressive political party. The family cut him off and mourned for him as if he were dead. Pierre was always a little afraid this might happen to him, so he carefully hid his true feelings from his parents. This ability to hide behind tact and courtesy worked both for and against Pierre in years to come.

Pierre was 15 years old in 1878, when the Paris Universal Exposition opened only a few blocks from his apartment on the rue Oudinot. He could walk over any time and see the wonders of the world and the advancements of science and technology on display. In the German pavilion, he saw a diorama (a display including figures and a painting) of an archaeological site in Greece. It represented a place called Olympia, and Pierre knew from his Greek textbooks that the site was important in understanding the ancient Greeks and how they worshipped.[3] At the time, the diorama was interesting to Pierre, but it was just one of many exhibits that made the exposition interesting.

At the age of 17, Pierre decided to enter the Saint Cyr military academy at Versailles, not far from

A diorama of ancient Olympia

Paris. He thought being an officer would be better than being a priest. But this idea lasted only a few months. Why learn to be an officer if France was not at war? Also, his friends among the young intellectuals belittled the military. Pierre decided he wanted a life of the mind more than a life in the barracks.

Pierre and many of his friends were glad to be called "Anglophiles"—lovers of English things. In the 1880s, the British seemed to be enjoying great success, whereas the French were struggling to recover from past misfortunes. Pierre dreamed of changing French society along British lines, or at least of modernizing the French way of doing things.

Young French Anglophiles had their clothes tailored the English way. They used English expressions when they talked, mixing them with French. They smoked pipes in order to look more English.

Pierre, going one step further, grew a huge "English" moustache, and he wore it for the rest of his life.

2

CHOOSING A PATH

A young man with no career—a young man secretly rebelling against his family's values but without a clear direction of his own—might pause, as Pierre did, to take his bearings and to see something of the world. What could be more natural for a wealthy young fellow than a trip abroad? And what foreign destination could suit Pierre more naturally than England? In 1883, at the age of 20, he set out across the English Channel. He carried letters written by his French friends to introduce him to important people in England, so Pierre was welcomed in many upper-class homes. He met influential Englishmen, including prime minister William Gladstone and future Nobel Peace Prize co-winner Austen Chamberlain.

Rugby was high on Pierre's list of places to visit in England. The school had hardly changed since *Tom Brown* was written, and Pierre was allowed to attend classes, to watch matches in cricket and soccer, and to talk informally with the students.

He also saw the game of rugby, a type of football

Opposite page: Pierre in his sports clothes

that had been invented at the school. What he didn't see was the rigid social system described in *Tom Brown's School Days.* Little boys "fagged," which meant they acted as servants for older boys. This servitude could be easy or unbearable, depending on the character of the older boy. The older boys had the privilege of dispensing punishments, which sometimes took the form of whippings. These practices had been greatly softened by 1883.

As if to see where a Rugby education might lead, the young baron also spent time at Oxford and at Cambridge, the two British universities where upper-class men finished their education.

Traveling among country houses in the Cotswold Hills near London, Pierre heard some local legends.

An artist's conception of the Cotswold Olympics, which were English in character rather than Greek.

COTSWOLD GAMES.

More than two centuries earlier, a landowner named Captain Robert Dover had wanted to irritate the super-religious Puritan government. Knowing that the Puritans disliked public amusements, Dover set up a program of rowdy games he called the Cotswold Olympics. The events included wrestling, fighting with sticks and swords, jumping, pitching logs, and throwing hammers.

The baron was fascinated by the idea. He knew about Olympics from his studies of Latin and Greek, but the Greek custom of athletic events dedicated to the gods had seemed remote from modern life. Yet Captain Dover had revived some of the Olympic tradition, and it sounded like a lot of fun.

When he pursued the legend, Pierre also learned about Dr. W. P. Brookes, who had staged country-style Olympics in Shropshire, England, beginning in 1840. In addition to the sporting contests, Brookes introduced heralds, marching bands, and literary competitions. The king of Greece heard about these "Olympic" games. Because Greece was the site of the ancient Olympics, he sent Brookes a silver urn to give as a prize to the winner of the five-event pentathlon—discus, javelin, short and long foot-races, and broad jump.

This story was too delightful to ignore. Coubertin wrote to Dr. Brookes and, during another trip to England in 1890, he traveled to Shropshire. He met Dr. Brookes and was made an honorary member of Brookes's Olympic Society. At this point, though, Pierre was just an observer. The idea of international games had not yet taken root in his mind. But it was nice to think that Olympic games could be played in rural England and could award a prize from the king of Greece. It supported an idea that Pierre had become very interested in: that Europe should develop links between countries and bring people together.

In the latter part of the 19th century, international cooperation was increasing in Europe and America. For instance, the Universal Postal Union allowed a stamp of one nation to carry a letter through many different countries to its destination. In another attempt to transcend national barriers, Dr. L. L. Zamenhof of Poland invented a new language, Esperanto, which borrowed from all the major European languages to create an easy-to-learn blend. Roads and railways crisscrossed Europe, and countries honored passports and travel tickets issued outside their borders. The rights of inventors and authors in one country were respected in others.

The name for all these developments was internationalism. Most French people didn't care for internationalism; they felt it would make them less French, less special, less patriotic. Pierre disagreed. He thought internationalism pointed to the future and that the French would be left behind unless they participated.

When he returned to Paris, Pierre tried to tell his father about his theories, but he met with angry opposition. His father was scandalized at the thought of his son trying to change French society. French society did not need a reformer, it needed a king!

Pierre would never openly defy his father. He loved him even if he was a hundred years behind the times. And Pierre knew how his family handled its black sheep. The ghost of his great-uncle haunted him at times like this.

Pierre had rejected the priesthood and the military as possible careers. Neither did he want to try to change society by becoming part of the existing government. His father was tired of Pierre's indecision. He didn't want to hear about Pierre wanting to travel, about Pierre needing to find himself, or about Pierre hanging around society drawing rooms. Pierre was to study law, and that was that.

In 1884, Pierre enrolled at the Sorbonne, a Paris university where the lectures were much more interesting than his old studies under the Jesuit fathers. But Baron Pierre still rebelled against his father in a quiet way—by skipping most of his law classes. He enjoyed lectures on the literature and history of ancient Greece and Rome. One lecturer was an American named Dr. William Milligan Sloane, whom Pierre knew personally. Sloane was about 10 years older than Pierre. During one of his many trips to

Dr. William Milligan Sloane

France, where he had relatives, he and Pierre met and became friends. Now that Sloane was a lecturer, Pierre was interested in learning from him.[4]

The Sorbonne was a traditional institution, the last place one would go to change French society. Since his work there didn't advance him toward this goal, Baron Pierre de Coubertin ignored his law classes and tried the life of a socialite. He became a frequent guest at the salons of aristocrats, where brilliant people came to share ideas and tea and to meet others with wealth and position. These people, Pierre found, were content with society as it was. But they were wealthy and influential. The baron treated them the same way he dealt with his father. He listened politely, and he never scoffed or sneered at ideas he thought were outdated or ill-conceived. Later, when Coubertin needed influential friends to further his dreams of founding international Olympic Games, he was glad he hadn't offended these people.

Still, Pierre wanted an occupation that would change society—especially upper-class society. Perhaps, he thought, he needed to know how to work with government. So in 1885, when he was 22, the young baron entered the Free School for Political Science, a private school that specialized in training people for government service. Here at last was a school where Pierre felt at home. He could "learn without a definite objective"[5]—that is, he had no examinations, no regular schedule of classes, no need to "pass" or get a good grade.

Since he had his own "Tom Brown" ideas about English and French methods of teaching, Pierre began to read books about theories of education. He found authors who agreed with him, many of whom admired the English system of school athletics the way Pierre did. They supported his idea that 11 hours a day of uninterrupted study made no sense. "An adolescent," Pierre wrote, "needs physical exercises: it is against nature to force him to be all brain."[6]

Pierre began to write articles and to lecture at meetings of the Society of Social Economy, a small group dedicated to change. This society became the baron's

An adolescent needs physical exercises: it is against nature to force him to be all brain.

model for how a group should be run. He used its procedures later when he organized the International Olympic Committee. In his speeches to the society, he tried to tie together his observations of English education and his views about internationalism.

Coubertin revisited England in 1887, and though he spoke excellent English, he attracted mostly French-speaking audiences. He spoke about the aims of the Society of Social Economy, about the changes they advocated: the reformation of France (and the world) into a free, great, and prosperous place without a violent revolution.

Eager to set the French government in motion, he returned to France and approached the Ministry of Public Instruction with some of his ideas. Most emphatically, he described the neglect of physical education in French *lycées* (high schools). The ministry took only enough notice to offer Pierre a small office, a small budget, and a huge mission: Find ways to improve French education.

It's possible government officials created the baron's job just so they could say they were doing something about education. But this little bit of official support inspired Pierre to work very hard over the next few years. He wrote hundreds of reports

Pierre (seated, third from left) worked closely with students and teachers at the École Monge.

on his research and ideas. He endorsed shorter classroom hours and urged teachers to pay more attention to analysis of ideas than to rote learning of facts. He advocated giving students chances to be leaders and allowing more time for athletics and games. He stressed the need for places to play— athletic fields, playgrounds and parks, lagoons and gymnasiums—none of which was a standard part of school design in France. The headmaster of one school, the École Monge, was especially progressive in his instructional methods, and Pierre easily persuaded him to try athletics as part of his program. The students thrived on the new system.

In the late 1880s, Coubertin's job took him throughout France. Visiting different schools, he compared their methods of education. Wherever physical education was available, the students seemed to work better, to pay closer attention for longer spans of time, and to retain facts and ideas better.

At one school, Pierre learned a favorite Latin motto of the headmaster, Father Didon. It was *Citius, Altius, Fortius,* which means "faster, higher, stronger." Worthy goals for athletes, Pierre thought. He stored the motto in a corner of his mind.

3

BUILDING ON THE PAST

When he'd done as much as he could do within the French government, Baron Pierre de Coubertin continued to work for education and athletics on his own. He tried to get powerful people interested in improving education in France. He made speeches and wrote articles, essays, and books.

To encourage interest in sports, he created the Union of French Athletic Sports Clubs, which became a power center for sport. As a "union," this group was able to advocate the interests of the sporting community. Coubertin even started a monthly newspaper, *The Athletic Review,* to stir up interest in sports. He wrote most of the articles himself.

By this time, the baron thought his speeches and articles might be boring people instead of inspiring them. He needed to capture the public's imagination and to stir up enthusiasm, but he had no idea how.

In 1889, Coubertin was commissioned by the Ministry of Public Instruction to visit North America and find out how high schools and colleges in the United

Opposite page: Many statues like this were uncovered during excavations at Olympia, revealing much about the ancient games.

States and Canada operated. He observed public and private schools, playground programs, and organized sports, and he liked what he saw. He even met a young politician he admired: Theodore Roosevelt. Here was a man, Pierre thought, who'd been educated properly. His body had developed along with his mind.

In Canada, he compared the French-type schools of Montreal with English-style schools in Toronto. In Pierre's opinion, the athletic boys at Ontario's English-system schools were more effectively educated than the students in Quebec's French-style schools.

As he traveled, Coubertin asked teachers about sports in their schools. What games did children play? Did rich children play the same games as poor children? How important were sports outside the schools? Did a game have the same rules wherever it was played?

The young baron made many friends in his travels. As he exchanged ideas with them, he realized he was part of a personal kind of internationalism. If people from many countries could take part in this kind of exchange, internationalism might more speedily achieve its goals of peace and unity.

And, since Coubertin was so involved with athletics, he naturally wondered whether sports contests could further the ideals of internationalism. Why not? International contests and matches would be a natural meeting ground for athletes of all countries. The aura of sportsmanship would lead to fellowship and friendship. It might lead to trade in ideas and in manufactured products.

But how? Every country played different games. Travel between countries was difficult and expensive. Telephone communication was in its infancy, and if competitors from two countries met, they were unlikely to speak the same language.

Back in France in 1889, Pierre visited the Paris Exposition, a world's fair much like the one he'd attended in 1878 and 1879—the one with the diorama of the ancient Greek city of Olympia. The excavations in Greece still interested the baron, and he must have known that many buildings had been

uncovered and reconstructed during the time between expositions. These were the very temples and meeting places used during the ancient Olympic games.

The highlight of the 1889 Paris Exposition was the new Eiffel Tower.

Baron de Coubertin, from his studies of Greek language and culture, knew the legends about the origins of the ancient Olympics. According to these tales, a Greek ruler, King Oenamaus, offered his daughter, Hippodamia, in marriage to the first man who could successfully kidnap her. That man would be king after Oenamaus.

A commoner named Pelops was the 14th man to accept the challenge. He found out that in each of the 13 previous abduction attempts, the king had driven a magnificent chariot to pursue his daughter and the kidnapper. No one had faster horses than Oenamaus. After catching the couple, Oenamaus always killed the young man.

Pelops was only a fair driver with an average chariot, so he bribed someone to weaken the axle that held

This early artwork depicts the story of Pelops and Hippodamia.

the wheels of the king's chariot. Pelops then kidnapped Hippodamia, and the king, as usual, sped after the young couple. This time, Oenamaus was killed when the sabotaged axle failed during the chase. When Pelops and Hippodamia were married, games and contests—the first Olympics—celebrated their wedding and the king's funeral at the same time.

The legend may be true, or the games at Olympia may have started as religious rites many years earlier. Ancient Greeks used animal sacrifices to worship their gods, until killing animals became unpopular. Then other rites were substituted. A musician might compose a song for the gods; a goldsmith might decorate part of a temple; an athlete like Pelops might dedicate a series of games to the gods.

Scholars have proof that Olympic games took place as early as 776 B.C. An ancient written record says that a cook named Corebus of Elis won a 200-meter (about 220-yard) race. The ancient games were held every four years, and prizes of money and laurel wreaths were given to winners.

Women were not allowed to compete at the games. If a woman even watched, she could be thrown from a cliff as punishment. Every five years women held rites of their own to worship Hera, the primary goddess of Greece, but the only athletic event was a 33-yard (30-meter) footrace.

The ancient Olympic rules, some of which have been discovered by archaeologists, had much more to do with religious duties than with sport. Athletes were supposed to train for 10 months before each set of Olympic games, and once a contestant had arrived at Olympia, he trained for another month with Olympic officials. Nothing but cheese and water was served at mealtimes.

It took money to be an Olympic athlete, even in ancient times. The 10 months of training were 10 months away from one's regular job—and regular pay. Expenses of the trip to Olympia were paid by the athlete or his family. If he entered the chariot race, he had to have his own vehicle and horses. And if he were lucky or skilled enough to win, he would have to provide a banquet to celebrate. Since very few athletic young men could afford all these expenses, many contestants depended on sponsors. Rich men, hoping the glory of a champion would be linked with their names, might support athletes while they trained.

After the Romans conquered Greece in 146 B.C., they continued to hold the games at Olympia. The last written record of an ancient Olympic competition states that an Armenian boxer named Varastad won a medal in A.D. 388—in the 291st games.

Shortly afterward, in 393, the Roman Emperor Theodosius I, who was a Christian, ordered the pagan worship site destroyed. Not long after that, an earthquake changed the course of the Alpheus River, and the temples and gymnasiums were covered with silt. By 403—only 15 years after the last set of ancient games—the ruins were completely buried.[7]

More than 13 centuries later, in 1764, an English minister named Richard Chandler visited Greece. An amateur archaeologist interested in ancient civilizations, he poked around Olympia with a Roman

Building on the Past

The ruins of the temple of Hera, where women's competitions were held

Coubertin's Olympics

The stadium of Olympia—site of the ancient games—once stood in this spot.

text for a guidebook. He found a thick wall topped by a rooflike structure.

Chandler told professional archaeologists about his find, so they would know where to dig to start their exploration of ancient Olympia's ruins. The discovery of the Olympic site caused a sensation in the Western world. Until that time, most scholars thought Olympic games were a pleasant myth, like ancient Greek stories about girls turning into trees or spiders or about men riding winged horses. Now it was clear that the games had been real, and more and more evidence about the religious life of ancient Greece was unearthed.

The excavation of Olympia went slowly at first. No real digging was done until 1829. Then, French scientists came to the site. They dug up parts of a temple and shipped them to the Louvre Museum in Paris.

The Greeks felt the French had stolen part of their national treasure. They were so angry that for years they wouldn't let anyone dig at Olympia—or anywhere else. But a team of German archaeologists who promised to uncover the ruins without taking

anything away from the site eventually won the Greek government's permission to uncover Olympia. Excavation started in 1875.

By 1889, many buildings had been uncovered, and scholars were able to piece together a re-creation of what Olympia had been like and of what had taken place there. The diorama Pierre saw at the Paris Universal Exposition showed temples with their statuary, a stadium, hotels and baths for spectators, shrines, treasuries, and administration buildings.

Baron de Coubertin realized that the ancient Olympics had a lot in common with his idea for athletic internationalism. Both brought athletes from various places together for friendly competition. Both were designed to glorify individual achievement instead of national identity. Both created an island of peace and friendship in the midst of conflict.

"Olympia," he wrote, "symbolizes an entire civilization, superior to cities, military heroes, and the ancient religions."[8]

If this superior civilization could be brought to life, political leaders and famous people would meet there. Friendships would be forged among athletes and leaders of many nations. Artists would come to paint and sculpt the athletes, and wonderful poems and songs would be written about them. Personal friendships would lead to international friendship. The threat of war would disappear.

Olympia was the catalyst Coubertin had been looking for—a way to create enthusiasm for a worldwide athletic movement that would lead to international understanding.

He began his campaign.

4

"YOUR HUMBLE SERVANT"

With his idea for a modern Olympics clear in his mind, Baron de Coubertin began to gather support. He didn't want support from the French government; it was notorious for not getting things done. In France, the way to make a change was to form a committee of private citizens. There were committees to influence almost every facet of public life, from postal rates to sanitation, theater to foreign exploration. Sometimes these committees were actually successful. So of course, Coubertin formed a committee.

He wrote and spoke in his most persuasive way to all his friends and acquaintances, asking them to support the goals of his Union of French Athletic Sports Clubs. Each time someone said yes, Coubertin added the new recruit's name to the union's stationery. Eventually, each letter he sent seemed to come from a group in which all the famous people in Paris were active members.

In November of 1892, Coubertin hosted a banquet to celebrate the fifth anniversary of the founding of

Opposite page: Pierre in his mid-30s

the Union of French Athletic Sports Clubs. It was held at the Sorbonne, the Paris university where he had once enrolled in law classes. In a speech to athletes, union members, educators, and politicians, he explained his idea.

> "Let us export oarsmen, runners, fencers...[so that] the cause of peace will have received a new and powerful support.... This thought is sufficient to encourage your humble servant to dream now of the second part of his program...the re-establishment of the Olympic games."[9]

By "your humble servant," Coubertin meant himself. He knew the value of presenting himself as the servant of an idea. If people thought he wanted glory for himself, he would lose support. Throughout most of his career, Coubertin named himself secretary of whatever group he created. This made it seem like he was acting for more important, busier men. Actually, as the secretary, he kept the power to run things.

Although this 1892 speech was a rousing one, few people understood what Pierre really meant. They thought he was talking about restoring the city of Olympia[10] and that Olympics was his fancy way of talking about amateur athletics. When they understood he was serious about staging modern contests, they taunted him about advocating that athletes compete in the nude, as was done in the ancient games. They also joked about him—horrors!—suggesting that cultivated Europeans compete with Asians and Africans.[11]

Marie Rothan

Pierre often described his vision—world peace through sport—to his family and their friends, but he rarely got any support from them. His parents thought he was a raging lunatic for even caring about anything but the French upper class. The only person in his circle who did not scoff was the daughter of some family friends. Her name was Marie Rothan, and she seemed to like and understand his ideas. She knew that, to him, Olympics meant a real event; the word was not just a fancy symbol in a confused philosophy. She took his side when the older people laughed at his idea.

Marie came to the Sorbonne to hear Pierre's speech. Later, she wrote him a letter praising his work. Soon the two were writing back and forth every day. Since Pierre had many associates and acquaintances but few close friends, the letters must have provided much-needed human contact outside his daily business.

In the autumn of 1892, through his Union of French Athletic Sports Clubs, Coubertin arranged his first international meet. A group of English rowers came to France for a boat race, and the French team won. Coubertin was thrilled—not only because of the French victory, but because this event showed that rules could be worked out to satisfy athletes of different nations.

Pierre relaxes aboard what appears to be a gondola months before starting the International Olympic Committee.

A statue of the explorer Christopher Columbus greets visitors to the Columbian Exposition held in Chicago, Illinois, in 1893.

The British wanted a rematch, and they invited the baron to bring a French team to race on the river Thames in the summer of 1893. Pierre accepted.

Immediately he was in trouble.

Three French rowing teams belonged to Coubertin's union, and they all demanded the right to go to England. Pierre got them to compromise by sending the best rowers from each team. He also persuaded the French team to play by British rules. Then the British claimed that not all the French team members were amateurs. To the French, someone could be an amateur athlete and still accept a cash prize. But if the athlete earned a living from sport, the term professional applied, and professionals were barred from amateur competitions. The British applied stricter rules: No amateur could accept cash prizes, and no laborer or tradesperson could compete. Coubertin used all his wit and charm to persuade the British to allow two working-class French rowers on the team.

Coubertin arranged other sporting meets in Paris in the 1890s. He combined them with parades, banquets, and ceremonies. He felt that modern events should be held as they were in ancient times, when every meet was accompanied by a feast or a funeral.

In late 1893, the government of France sent Coubertin to Chicago for the Columbian Exposition, a huge world's fair celebrating the 400th anniversary of Columbus's voyages. When his official work was done, Pierre spoke at several universities in the United States.

He visited his old friend Dr. William Milligan Sloane, who was teaching French history at the College of New Jersey in Princeton, which was renamed Princeton University in 1896. Dr. Sloane was the first distinguished person to catch Pierre's spark of enthusiasm for the revival of international Olympic games. Sloane was no athlete, but he enjoyed a good contest, and he was delighted by the prospect of restoring something from the ancient civilizations he had studied.

Pierre stayed with Sloane for three weeks, and Sloane helped him clarify his thoughts and plans for

Amateurism

Pierre de Coubertin and his friends were obsessed with the idea of amateurism, thinking that an athlete's motives were important to the ideals of sportsmanship. Anyone motivated by money, they argued, could not have the same love of sport as those who played strictly for the joy of competing.

The Olympic founders might have been right, but the world has undergone a lot of change, and the Olympics have changed with it. Recently, professional tennis and basketball players, who have earned a lot of money playing their sports, have participated in the Olympics.

They could, because in 1981 the IOC repealed Rule 26 of the Olympic Charter, which required strict proof of amateurism. The rule was often challenged. Manufacturers of sporting goods frequently donated clothing and equipment to athletes in return for the prestige—and the free publicity—of having their products used by Olympic athletes. Were these free items a form of payment? Were athletes from Eastern Europe, who were supported and trained with funds from their countries' budgets, still amateurs? Questions like these constantly plagued the IOC.

With the repeal, the job of deciding who would be eligible to compete in the Olympics fell to the international federation (IF) of individual sports.

Jim Thorpe was stripped of his track-and-field medals when officials learned he had played baseball for money. Seventy years later, however, the IOC restored his medals.

Some IFs demanded that athletes who earned money have it placed in trust funds. They could draw on these funds for support, but would remain eligible to compete as amateurs. The International Tennis Federation decided that any player under the age of 20 was an amateur, no matter how much money he or she had earned.

Track stars like Carl Lewis, Edwin Moses, and Mary Decker Slaney earned thousands of dollars in appearance fees each time they raced, but were allowed to compete in the Olympics.

Delegates to the congress would iron out all the questions of amateur sports and decide how to restore the Olympic Games.

restoring the Games.[12] He arranged for Coubertin to speak about the Olympics at a club for graduates of the College of New Jersey. The audience was polite, but no one seemed excited about his proposal.

The two friends continued to refine the plan, and by the time Pierre returned to Paris, he knew how he was going to proceed. He would convene an international congress of people interested in amateur sports, and this congress would form yet another committee. Delegates to the congress would iron out all the questions of amateur sports and decide how to restore the Olympic Games. He had drawn up the program with Sloane, and the two of them had decided how to word the invitations.[13] Later, Pierre wrote that Sloane was his only "counsel and confidant in all this business."[14]

When Pierre got back to France, he heard that the government was preparing to hold another world's fair in Paris in 1900. What a wonderful way, Pierre thought, to introduce an international Olympics. Even if the French weren't interested in sports—and they weren't—sports fans and organizers from other countries would like the chance to attend an international meet in Paris. And they could see the fair at the same time.

Invitations went out from Dr. Sloane to English-speaking sports enthusiasts and educators who might be interested in attending Coubertin's conference. They were signed by Coubertin, Sloane, and Charles Herbert, the president of the British Athletic Association. Pierre de Coubertin sent invitations, which he alone signed, to speakers of French-speaking people interested in sports and education.[15]

Professor Sloane had agreed to be an officer of this conference, and so did important men from England, Hungary, and Sweden. No men from the working class—and no women at all—were included in any phase of this congress.

Since hardly anyone had yet caught Pierre's excitement about modern Olympics, he didn't tell the delegates his real purpose. Instead, his program said they'd be discussing general questions of international sport, such as:

- Can an athlete earn money from a sport and still be an amateur?
- If an athlete earns money in one sport, can he be considered an amateur in another?
- Can a laborer be considered an amateur?
- Can money be given as a prize?
- If an object (like a medal) is given as a prize, how much should it be worth?
- Can organizers charge an admission fee?
- Who gets the profits from admission fees—the athletes, the organizers, the clubs where the athletes train, or someone else?
- Should betting among the spectators be allowed?

To all these questions, Pierre de Coubertin added one more—and placed it near the end of the program where it would not be easily noticed:

How can we re-establish the Olympic Games?

5

SWITCHING BABIES

History is always interested in "firsts." Pierre de Coubertin wanted the first modern Olympics to take place in Paris. If the Olympics were a success, Paris would always be honored as the first host city. This honor was a gift Pierre wanted to give to the city he loved.

To bring this honor to Paris, Coubertin had to forget that modern Olympics had already been held. The Cotswold and Shropshire Olympics were easy to forget; few people knew about them. More importantly, however, he had to ignore four sets of games held in Greece between 1859 and 1888.

The 1859 Olympics were held to celebrate Greek independence from the Turks, who had ruled them since the 1300s. The money for these games was given by a rich Greek named Evangelios Zappas, so they were called the Zappeion Olympics. All the events were track and field—that is, running, jumping, and throwing contests. All the athletes were Greek, and every prize was some amount of money.

Opposite page: The Zappeion Palace in Athens

The organizers hadn't set up any seats for the audience. The playing field was on the same level as the spectators, so people couldn't see what was going on. During the contests, the crowd, trying to see, inched farther and farther forward, until they crowded onto the track. Police tried to push them back. Fights started, and arrests were made. Even some athletes were arrested!

Zappas died shortly after these games, but he left his fortune in a trust fund to pay for future Zappeion games. With this money, a second Zappeion Olympics was held in 1870 and a third in 1875. The site of the 1875 games was the Panathenaic Stadium, an ancient structure that had been partially excavated by archaeologists. The prizes were olive branches, bouquets of flowers, and (again) money.

Spectators sat on the sides of a steep-sided ravine; the playing field was at the bottom. Officials in tailcoats and top hats tried to set an example of dignified behavior, but the spirit of the crowds was definitely undignified. Enthusiastic spectators argued about athletes and events—and got into wrestling and boxing matches of their own. During these informal matches, the fighters rolled downhill, and everyone in front of them rolled down too, sometimes into the path of the runners.

Among those who won cash prizes at the Zappeion Olympics were a stonecutter, a butcher, and a handyman. People in Greece started arguing about whether laborers, who might be motivated by the chance to win money, should be allowed to compete. Many people felt that earning money from sport made the athlete a professional, and this wasn't in the spirit of the ancient Olympics. Others said they didn't want Greece to be like England and France, where only wealthy gentlemen could afford to be sportsmen.

Amateurism was argued on all sides throughout the life of the Zappeion Olympics. Who should compete? Was love of sport—not glory or prize money—the only reason to enter the Games? What had the ancient Greek rules been? Could ancient rules be used in modern times?

Pierre de Coubertin was smart enough to use these issues to lure guests to his "International Congress of Amateurs." Luckily for their host, only a few delegates had heard of the Zappeion Olympics, but all of them agreed that amateur sports had to get organized.

The baron had to work hard to get people to attend his congress. He sent many duplicate invitations, and he wrote letters to remind people that they had been invited. He had to assure and reassure people that their points of view would be represented, and he urged them to set aside their prejudices. For instance, the French delegate from an important gymnastics club refused to come if Germans were invited. Germany was a powerful European country; Pierre wasn't sure people would believe the congress was truly international without its support.

Finally, one German agreed to come, but only as an observer. Since the German was not an official delegate, the French gymnastics delegate also came.

The program from Pierre's International Congress of Amateurs

CONGRÈS INTERNATIONAL ATHLÉTIQUE DE PARIS

16 - 24 Juin 1894

Le Congrès a été convoqué par l'*Union des Sociétés Françaises de Sports Athlétiques* dans le but d'étudier la question de l'**Amateurisme** et de faire un premier effort dans la voie de l'**unification** des règlements de Sports : ainsi se trouvera préparé, pour un avenir assez proche, le rétablissement des **Jeux Olympiques** sur des bases et dans des conditions conformes aux nécessités de la vie moderne.

Les Commissaires organisateurs du Congrès étaient

pour la FRANCE ET L'EUROPE CONTINENTALE: M. le baron Pierre de Coubertin, Secrétaire général de l'Union des Sports Athlétiques ;
pour l'ANGLETERRE ET LES COLONIES ANGLAISES: M. C. Herbert, Secrétaire de l'Amateur Athletic Association d'Angleterre ;
pour le CONTINENT AMÉRICAIN : M. W. M. Sloane, Professeur à l'Université de Princeton (États-Unis).

LE CONGRÈS S'OUVRIRA LE SAMEDI SOIR 16 JUIN 1894
au Palais de la Sorbonne à Paris
ET DURERA 8 JOURS

Il sera présidé par :
M. le BARON DE COURCEL, Sénateur, ancien Ambassadeur.

Les Vice-Présidents sont :
M. M. Le Vicomte Léon de JANZÉ, Président de l'Union des Sports Athlétiques.
Sir John ASTLEY, Président du Sports Club de Londres.
George A. ADEE, Président de l'University Athletic Club de New-York.
G. de SAINT-CLAIR, ancien président de l'Union des Sports Athlétiques.
M. KETELS, Président de la Fédération Belge des Sociétés de Courses à pied.
le Capitaine BALCK, Professeur à l'Institut central de Gymnastique de Stockholm.
G. STREHLY, Professeur au Lycée Montaigne.
F. KÉMÉNY, Directeur de l'Ecole Royale d'Eger (Hongrie).

Les Commissaires sont :
M. M. le Baron Pierre de COUBERTIN, Commissaire général, 20, rue Oudinot, Paris.
C. HERBERT, Secrétaire de l'Amateur Athletic Association, 10 John St (Adelphi), Londres.
le Comte Jacques de POURTALÈS, 7, rue Tronchet, Paris,
Franz REICHEL, Commissaire de la Presse, 9, rue Royer Collard, Paris.
A. de la FRÉMOIRE, 7, Place Malesherbes, Paris.
le Vicomte de MADEC, 83, Boulevard de Courcelles, Paris.

Les fêtes qui seront données à l'occasion du Congrès, comprendront :
1° Une fête de Longue Paume au Jardin du Luxembourg, le dimanche 17 juin.
2° Une fête d'Escrime, le mardi 19 juin.
3° Une fête de nuit, le jeudi 21 juin.
4° Une fête nautique, le dimanche 24 juin.

◀ PROGRAMME ▶

Amateurisme et Professionalisme

I. — Définition de l'amateur: bases de cette définition. — Possibilité et utilité d'une définition Internationale.
II. — Suspension, disqualification et requalification. — Des faits qui les motivent et des moyens de les vérifier.
III. — Est-il juste de maintenir une distinction entre les différents sports au point de vue amateuriste, spécialement pour les courses de chevaux (gentlemen) et le tir aux pigeons ? — Peut-on être professionnel dans un sport et amateur dans un autre ?
IV. — De la valeur des objets d'art donnés en prix. — Est-il nécessaire de limiter cette valeur ? — Quelles mesures doit-on prendre contre celui qui vend l'objet d'art gagné par lui ?
V. — Légitimité des ressources provenant des admissions sur le terrain. — Cet argent peut-il être partagé entre les sociétés ou entre les concurrents; peut-il servir d'indemnité de déplacement ? — Dans quelle limite des équipiers peuvent-ils être indemnisés, soit par la société adverse soit par leur propre société ?
VI. — La définition générale de l'amateur peut-elle s'appliquer également à tous les sports ? — Comporte-t-elle des restrictions spéciales en ce qui concerne la vélocipédie, l'aviron, les sports athlétiques, etc. ?...
VII. — Du pari. — Est-il compatible avec l'amateurisme ? — Des moyens d'en arrêter le développement.

Jeux Olympiques

VIII. — De la possibilité de leur rétablissement. — Avantages au point de vue de l'athlétisme et au point de vue moral et international.
IX. — Conditions à imposer aux concurrents. — Sports représentés. — Organisation matérielle, périodicité des jeux olympiques rétablis, etc....
X. — Nomination d'un Comité International chargé d'en préparer le rétablissement.

Règlement du Congrès

Les Unions et les Sociétés qui participeront au Congrès ne seront pas liées par les résolutions adoptées. Le congrès a pour but d'émettre des avis sur les différentes questions qui lui seront soumises et de préparer, mais non d'établir une législation Internationale.
    Les mémoires écrits en Français seront reçus au Secrétariat général jusqu'au 10 Juin, les mémoires écrits en langues étrangères, jusqu'au 1er Juin seulement. Ils seront classés en deux catégories selon qu'ils émaneront de personnalités individuelles ou de Sociétés. L'envoi de mémoires ou de communications est libre : nulle condition n'est exigée, mais les sociétés devront, en tous les cas, joindre à leurs envois le texte des règlements qui les régissent. Tout mémoire qui ne traiterait pas de l'une des questions inscrites au programme ci-joint, sera rigoureusement écarté.
    Des cartes donnant entrée dans la salle des séances seront à la disposition des personnes qui en feront la demande avant le 10 Juin en justifiant de leur désir de prendre part au Congrès. Les Sociétés pourront se faire représenter par des Délégués. Elles devront en ce cas, en donner avis avant le 10 Juin.

Toutes les communications doivent être adressées à M. le **Baron Pierre de COUBERTIN,** Commissaire-général, **20, Rue Oudinot, PARIS.**

By the time the congress began, Pierre had acceptances from 79 delegates from 12 countries, as well as many honorary patrons who supported his efforts but did not appear. These sponsors included the kings of Greece and Belgium, the Prince of Wales, the crown prince of Sweden, and Grand Duke Vladimir of Russia, as well as many commoners.

Most of the delegates were connected with sport in some way. Others were lawyers, educators, and members of international peace networks. Some delegates became prominent in Olympic history—especially those from Sweden, the United States, and Greece: Victor Balk, William Milligan Sloane, and Demetrios Bikelas, respectively.

When the delegates arrived, they were surprised to read on their tickets that they were at a "Congress for the Re-establishment of the Olympic Games" instead of an "International Congress of Amateurs." By changing the tickets and placing the emphasis on re-establishing the Olympics, Pierre managed to make the Olympics the main focus of the congress. Later, he bragged quietly about how he had "switched babies" on such a large group of distinguished men. He called it one of his "little deceptions."[16]

Just before the congress began, Coubertin published an article in the *Revue de Paris*, listing the principles important for modern Olympic Games:

Victor Balk

1. Games should be held every four years, as they were in ancient Greece.
2. The events should consist of modern sports.
3. Only adults should compete.
4. Athletes should not be paid or rewarded with money.
5. Each set of Games should be held in a different country, so they will be truly international.

Demetrios Bikelas

These principles were presented as though they had already been voted on and accepted. In the same article, Coubertin announced that the first Games would be held in Paris in 1900.[17]

At last, on June 23, 1894, at the Sorbonne, Coubertin called his international meeting to order. The motto for his congress was *Citius, Altius, Fortius,* the words he'd heard from Father Didon, who delivered the benediction for the congress.

Of the 2,000 people who attended the opening banquet, only 79 were delegates. Pierre fed them well, and he had them listen to speeches, poems, and a special performance of the "Delphic Hymn to Apollo," a piece of music from ancient Greece that had recently been deciphered by archaeologists. The words and music of this piece were both ancient, but the modern composer Gabriel Fauré had adapted the music for an orchestra and chorus. The main melody was carried by a soprano soloist.

This musical piece was probably the reason why so many people attended the banquet. Coubertin had gotten every bit of publicity that such a performance could command. People were curious about how a tune written 2,000 years earlier would sound.

Later, Pierre described the moment in his *Olympic Memoirs:*

> A sort of subtle emotion flowed as the ancient eurythmy sounded across the distance of the ages. Hellenism [the ancient Greek spirit] thus infiltrated the vast enclosure. In these first hours, the Congress had come to a head. Henceforth I knew, consciously or not, that no one would vote against the restoration of the Olympic Games.[18]

This elaborate banquet was only the first in a long line of feasts. Coubertin knew how to win the delegates' favor. He kept them fed and entertained at luncheons, pageants, and parades. At banquets, delegates were filled with rich food and sweets while they chatted with Pierre's aristocratic French friends. Their wine glasses were kept full. Musicians played and sang.

Sometimes, to get his way, the baron would schedule a long, boring speech—and then call for a vote

Coubertin's Olympics

During Pierre's lifetime, activities like competitive rowing were considered gentlemen's sports.

on an important question. The delegates, weary with talk and tired of sitting still, usually voted for whatever the baron wanted.

The money to pay for the opening banquet and concert came from Coubertin's own pocket. At the time, he had a great deal of money, and by paying, he could have everything his own way. If he'd tried to get money from the government, he would have had to fill out dozens of forms and ask permission for every little thing. That wasn't the baron's style.

The delegates paid a fee to attend the congress, and they paid their own traveling and hotel expenses. The baron saw to it that they got their money's worth.[19]

The congress split into two committees—one for amateurism and the other for the Olympics. The members of the congress never did vote on whether

to revive the games. They just went ahead with plans for how best to manage them.

The Committee on Amateurism decided not to allow cash prizes and ruled that no athlete could be paid for training. The committee members didn't discuss which social class an athlete should come from. It was obvious to them that if one couldn't win money or be paid for training, then only gentlemen could afford to compete. These rules were to apply to all competitions, not just those at the Olympic level.

The Committee on Amateurism made its report on June 24, the second day of the congress[20] and then ceased to exist. The rules written by this short-lived gathering of gentlemen remain controversial even a century later.

The Committee on Olympics started out with only five members: Demetrios Bikelas from Greece, Victor Balk from Sweden, Charles Herbert from England, William Milligan Sloane from the United States, and Pierre de Coubertin from France. Their first meeting was informal; they had fled to Bikelas's apartment to get away from the hectic atmosphere at the Sorbonne.[21] These five decided that each would take the presidency for four years—an "Olympiad"—at the end of which he would produce a meet of Olympic Games.

Balk was prepared to be first, with Games in 1900. He had told Pierre this at least two weeks before the congress started,[22] and the baron was not happy about it. He wanted the 1900 Games for Paris.

The five members of the Committee on the Olympics renamed themselves the International Olympic Committee (IOC), and this is still the name of the committee that oversees the Olympics. The original 1894 committee adopted some general rules for conducting the Games, drew up a list of possible events, and decided that athletes and countries must live up to "Olympic ideals." If a country wouldn't or couldn't observe these standards, it could be excluded from the Games.

At the final sessions of the congress, Baron de Coubertin got his way about everything. The rules he described in his earlier article in the *Revue de Paris* were the rules the congress adopted. No one argued. No one tried to change his wording or his meaning.

Coubertin was delighted.

By this time, the delegates were excited about the Olympics. After talking about international games for so many days, they could hardly wait to see their ideas come to life. They brought up the question of when and where to hold the first Olympics.

Stories have been written about how Coubertin "saved" the 1900 Olympics for Paris, instead of letting it go to Stockholm, Sweden, as IOC member Balk proposed. Most say that Pierre was suddenly inspired to hold a quick conference with Bikelas of Greece and then to propose that the six-year wait was too long and that Athens should be the site of Games in 1896.

But it probably didn't happen like that. Balk had been discussing a 1900 Stockholm Olympics since he arrived in Paris, so Pierre would not have been surprised to hear Stockholm proposed. The matter must have been settled by the five original IOC members, perhaps at the meeting in Bikelas's apartment.[23] Coubertin usually took careful minutes of every meeting, and the minutes of the congress are available for anyone to read.[24] If the decision for Athens instead of Stockholm had been made at a formal meeting, the minutes would mention it. But no one recorded what went on during that very informal afternoon at Bikelas's.

All organizations have officers, and the IOC was to be no exception. The members decided that the president should be from the country where the next Games were to be played. Therefore, Bikelas was the first president of the IOC. Coubertin was the secretary, and Sloane was the vice president. For 1900, the presidency would pass to Coubertin, for 1904 to Sloane, for 1908 to Herbert, and for 1912 to Balk. The five original IOC members were sure that, by 1912, more countries would be represented on the IOC and would be eager to hold Games.[25]

Before and during the Sorbonne congress, Coubertin was so eager to make certain things happen that he almost willed them into being. He would announce a topic for discussion, and his own ideas would guide the conversation in ways that eventually gave him exactly what he expected.

On June 23, 1894, Coubertin confidently announced to at least 14 men that they had been chosen for membership in the International Olympic Committee. He was convinced that anyone asked would feel honored and would serve. While no one actually said no, a few—such as Italian member Lucchesi Palli—resigned later that year.[26]

Switching Babies

6

WHOSE OLYMPICS ANYWAY?

Now that his Olympic idea was accepted, Pierre de Coubertin realized he couldn't organize every single detail of the first Games himself. He had to trust Bikelas to arrange things in Athens, and he could only hope the Greeks would find money to put on the Games. Bikelas, himself a historian, knew people in high places in Greece and proved himself at once by obtaining the patronage of King George of Greece, and his sons, Crown Prince Constantine and Princes George and Nicholas.

Pierre gave what help he could from Paris. His most important and lasting contribution was organizing and structuring the International Olympic Committee.

As the first secretary of the IOC, Coubertin met with experts in various sports. They decided how long each race should be, what equipment was needed, and how any disagreements would be settled. Scoring systems were developed for events, like wrestling and fencing, that had no distance or time measurements.

Opposite page: The royal pavilion for the 1896 Games. Coubertin is not in this picture. He had been effectively excluded from prominence by the Athenian Organizing Committee.

The International Olympic Committee

Members of the first International Olympic Committee

The IOC was, and still is, a group of private citizens. Coubertin specifically planned it that way. If members represented countries, politicians might give seats on the committee as rewards to their friends or political supporters.

As private citizens, the members of the IOC, free from the need for government approval, can dictate how the Games will be played. For example, without bothering about relations between, say, Iceland and other countries, they can say, "The Games will be in Iceland. If you don't like it, don't come."

The committee likes to remind people that its members represent the IOC in their home countries. They don't represent their countries at the IOC.

The only way to become a member of the IOC is to be invited by those who already belong. New members are considered only when an old member has resigned or died. An IOC member has to be well known as a supporter of amateur athletics. Members may stay with the IOC until they are 72 years old; they cannot be dismissed. The committee's purpose is to encourage amateur sport and to decide general policy matters for the Games. Questions about amateurism, drug testing, commercial sponsors, and future Olympic sites are among the many concerns governed by the IOC.

Together, Pierre and his advisors worked out instructions for athletes, judges, and coaches in each event. These directives were sent to Greece and were eventually printed up and passed along to the organizer of each team. Even though few competitors knew modern Greek, that was the language in which the rules were printed. Most teams took one look and tossed out the rulebook. They didn't need rules to tell them how to run or jump or swim. Later, arguments over rules were difficult to settle.

While he worked on the Games, Pierre was thinking about marrying Marie Rothan, the woman he'd been writing to for two years. She seemed to share his dream for the Olympics. He could certainly support a wife and family, especially since he planned to go on living in his parents' home, which offered all the stylish necessities of life.

In October, Pierre and Marie announced their engagement. Pierre's parents were horrified. It was one thing to be friendly with a middle-class family, but one did not want them for relations. Besides, Marie was an "old maid" of 33, older than Pierre by 2 years. And worst of all to Pierre's Catholic parents, Marie was a Protestant.

But Pierre had always rebelled against his parents' conservative views. He never believed, as they did, that France should be ruled by a king. He never agreed that boys were best educated by priests who never let them move from their desks. He never believed that holding Olympic Games in modern times was a fool's dream. He tactfully brushed aside all objections to his marriage.

Pierre probably was not deeply in love with Marie. He was romantic only in his ideas about international sport and world peace through physical fitness. Marie, Pierre felt, was a mature woman who would share his ideas and encourage his schemes. Her letters to him were certainly admiring and supportive.

This busy interval before the first Olympics might not have been the best time for Pierre to make major decisions about his personal life. Perhaps Marie was the one who suggested marriage and Pierre just went along with the idea. If this were the case, Marie may have hoped to be the "first lady of the Olympics" and to share the glory she foresaw coming to Pierre.

Before he could marry, bad news came from Greece. Bikelas and the IOC had counted on being allowed to use the money that Evangelios Zappas had left to put on more Zappeion Olympics. But the people in charge of that money would not release it. Despite the king's patronage of the IOC event, they maintained that their money was only for Zappeion Olympics.

Bikelas and his Athenian Olympic Committee could not find another source of money, and time was short. Coubertin sailed for Greece at once to see if he could help Bikelas get the project back on track and generate the enthusiasm that brings in large contributions.

In Athens, he found poor and jobless people. Their government didn't seem able to get anything done. But Pierre wanted to save his Olympic dream. He decided that the Greek people needed the Olympics. The project would create many jobs and give them pride in their country.

All he had to do was convince the Greeks.

Through an interpreter, the baron gave an interview to newspaper reporters. He said, "We French have a proverb that says that there is no French word for 'impossible.' I have been told this morning that 'impossible' is a Greek word. I do not believe it."[27] In this way, he made the Games a challenge to Greek pride.

Since Bikelas and the IOC couldn't get anything done, Coubertin decided to create a new group, the Olympic Organizing Committee (OOC). All the members of the OOC would be Athenians who knew how to get things done in their city. They would carry out the wishes of the IOC. To lead the OOC, Coubertin recruited the one person everyone would respect: Constantine, the crown prince of Greece.

Prince Constantine was acting as regent—temporary ruler—while his father was away attending the funeral of the czar of Russia. It would not be easy for

Prince Constantine

an unknown foreigner to claim any of the prince's time. But Coubertin knew Alex Mercati, the son of an important banker. Mercati was also a boyhood friend of the prince; he arranged an audience.

Constantine saw advantages in becoming head of Pierre's OOC. The people of Greece would have a chance to watch him, their future king, accomplish the impossible. Also, he would be linked closely with Greek patriotism. The Greek royal family was actually Danish—placed on the Greek throne by a coalition of European rulers—and some Greeks resented them as foreign impostors. A Greek project like the Olympics would make Constantine and his family seem more Greek.

Constantine and his two brothers, Nicholas and George, took over the job of raising money to put on the Games.

Coubertin went everywhere in Athens. He talked to important people and ordinary people. He told the officials what the cab drivers thought of the Olympics, and he told the flower vendors what the politicians were doing to help or hurt the Games. He finally got a written promise from the Greek prime minister, who had opposed the Games: Even though the government couldn't financially support the Games, it would not try to prevent them.

Members of the first International Olympic Committee with the members of the Greek Olympic Organizing Committee. Coubertin is in the back row, fourth from right.

After three weeks, Pierre felt he had done all he could. But before he returned to Paris, he made his own pilgrimage to the site of ancient Olympia.

He arrived at the closest town, Pyrgos, toward nightfall. In his memoirs, Pierre recalls that, eager to see the sacred ruins, he woke before dawn. The buildings were small and crowded together, but he was inspired by what had taken place there, and his feelings "magnified every dimension."[28]

Coubertin stayed several days, walking among the ruins, picnicking by the Alpheus River, and generally meditating on what had gone on and what was to come. His writings tell of how he imagined famous ancient Greeks going about their usual business of philosophy, democracy, and art. The baron's written language is flowery and full of stilted phrasing—he would not have spoken the same way—but it is clear that he was deeply and emotionally involved with the site.

Nevertheless, he couldn't stay forever; his future bride was waiting for him in Paris. He had to go

*Pierre and Marie in a
photograph taken
around the time of their
marriage*

home. Marie and Pierre were married in a Protestant ceremony on March 12, 1895. They moved
into the family apartment on the rue Oudinot, but
after only three weeks, they went to live with Marie's
mother, whom they always called "Madame." Their
home was with her until her death.[29]

The baron tried to go back to work on the Olympics. But he found that Prince Constantine wanted
to run things without help from outside Greece. The
prince was able to raise large amounts of money
from donors in Greece and from Greeks living outside their country. One of these expatriates, George
Averoff, sent one million drachmas—a huge sum—
from his home in Alexandria, Egypt. The donation
assured the IOC that the Games would truly be
played. His money was reserved for the restoration
of a stadium.[30]

More money was raised from the sale of special
postage stamps anticipating the Games. Revenue
from postage is still an important source of financ-
ing for the modern Games.

Since he had raised all the money, Prince Constantine felt he was now firmly in charge of the
Games. The IOC and its secretary were not welcome
to make decisions—or even suggestions—about the
Games. But Coubertin had engineered the Sorbonne
congress. Coubertin had motivated the Greek nation to support the Olympics. How could they brush
him aside now?

Unable to understand how his Greek colleagues
could turn against him, he wrote repeatedly to both
Bikelas and Prince Constantine. He had never sought
glory for himself, but it would have been nice to
have glory thrust upon him. If not glory, at least
recognition. If not recognition, at least a simple nod
of thanks. Instead, Pierre was refused, rebuffed,
and ignored.

Coubertin tried to help the Greeks find a plan for
building a velodrome—an arena for bicycle races.
While he was searching, he learned that Prince Constantine was already building one from a Danish
design.

The baron also tried to help by hiring an artist,

*The Greek OOC placed
a statue of George
Averoff at the entrance
to the Panathenaic
Stadium. Without his
donation, the 1896
Games might not have
been held.*

Coubertin's Olympics

The stadium of Lycurgus under reconstruction for the first modern Olympic Games

The two sides of the medals given at the 1896 Games

Jules Chaplain from France, to design a medal for the winners. Pierre envisioned three medals for each event being cast from this design—one in gold, one in silver, and one in bronze. Prince Constantine insisted that only one medal per event be given, and that was to be silver.

In those days, gold coins were spent every day. A gold medal might have seemed like a cash prize. Perhaps, too, the Greeks were looking for ways to save money. Finally, the planners of the Games agreed that the winner in each event would get a silver medal and that the prize for second place would be a bronze medal. Arguments about who won "the gold" at the first Olympics can be settled with one word: nobody.

The majority of Olympic events were planned for the Panathenaic Stadium in the middle of Athens. This site had been used by the ancient Romans when they ruled Greece. They called it the stadium of Lycurgus. While rebuilding the stadium's wooden understructure for the Games, construction workers found tunnels through which wild animals had entered the arena for the circuses that had entertained the Roman-ruled Greeks. Later, the Turks who ruled Greece had stripped all the white marble from the arena walls. Now, the Olympic Organizing Committee decided to rebuild the understructure, install new marble facings, and create marble thrones for the royal family. The one thing they couldn't rebuild was the runners' track.

From an athlete's point of view, the stadium had a bad track. The oval was too narrow—later, the athletes called it "the cigar"[31]—forcing the runners to make tight, hazardous turns. If the builders tried to widen the track, they would have had to remove many rows of seats. The OOC could have moved the outside walls apart or built a new facility elsewhere, but the budget could not be stretched. The Greeks decided the athletes would have to live with the bad track.

The IOC assigned one task specifically to the baron: He was to send invitations asking athletic clubs, universities, sports federations, and others to participate in the Games. The job was not handled well. Despite

One drawback of the stadium was the sharp turn runners would have to make.

*The govern-
ment laughed
at the baron
when he sug-
gested that
tax money
should pay for
transportation
and lodging
for a team.*

all his organizational skills and all his devotion to the idea of the Games, Coubertin almost ruined everything by making foolish mistakes.

For example, when he sent invitations and rules to England, he carelessly sent copies written in French. Also, many invitations went astray in England; they didn't reach the two most important sources of British athletes, the athletic clubs at Oxford and Cambridge universities. Partly because of this slip-up, the team from England turned out to be a South African hurdler, a British tourist, an Australian, and two members of the staff of the British embassy in Athens.

The Germans were expected to send a strong team to Athens, but a newspaper reported that the "Renovator," Pierre de Coubertin, had said he was glad the Germans hadn't been at the Sorbonne congress and glad they wouldn't come to Athens. Coubertin scrambled to publish his side of the story—that he never said such things and that they were contrary to the Olympic spirit—in the German press. He enlisted the help of the German IOC member, who helped cool things down. An international incident was averted, but the Germans sent only a turner-type gymnastics team to Athens.[32]

The Belgians and the Dutch would not participate unless their athletes were paid, so neither Belgium nor the Netherlands fielded a team.

Coubertin's invitations to French athletes did not contain careless or foolish errors. They reached the right people. But the invitations were simply ignored by most sporting clubs. The government laughed at the baron when he suggested that tax money should pay for transportation and lodging for a team. When the Games began, two cyclists, some fencers, and a long-distance runner made up the entire French team.

Throughout 1895, paperwork—Olympic bulletins, tentative programs, royal edicts, committee instructions—flowed from Athens to Coubertin, who was still secretary of the IOC. None of the material mentioned the baron's name. It was as though the Greeks were trying to forget he had any part in the Games. Pierre tried to remind the world of his place in the project by writing letters to the editors of various newspapers. The Greeks answered by calling him "a thief, seeking to rob Greece of her inheritance."[33]

In his memoirs, Coubertin described this difficult period in his relationship with the Greeks:

> Sure of success, they had no more need of me; I was no more than an intruder recalling by my presence the foreign initiative. From this moment on, not only was my name no longer mentioned but each one appeared to make it his business to help efface [wipe away] the memory of the part played by France in the restoration of the Olympiads. Most of those whom, the year before, I had gathered around the newborn work avoided meeting me or affected [pretended] not to recognize me.[34]

Pierre de Coubertin and his bride arrived in Athens early in April of 1896. His name was on the list of honored guests, but his title was not "Secretary of the IOC." It was not "Renovator," or "Father of the Modern Olympics." He was simply called a "journalist."

If Coubertin was disappointed, he hid it well.

7

"THIS MARVELOUS RESULT"

In the United States, Professor William Sloane faced his own set of problems. How does one person, living in a time before long-distance telephones, faxes, or computer networks, spread news across a country the size of the United States? Who should he tell that Olympic Games will be held? How could he recruit American athletes to compete?

Nowadays, ordinary kids in gyms and swimming pools throughout the world have seen the Olympics on television. Many young athletes dream of Olympic glory. They beg their parents and teachers for the chance to learn how to do a handstand on a balance beam or how to vault a 21-foot-high horizontal bar.

But in 1894, when Pierre de Coubertin asked Professor Sloane to find and train American athletes for his Olympics in Greece, no one knew what Olympics meant. The Sorbonne congress had not made the front page in U.S. newspapers. It hadn't even made the most obscure page of the sports section.

All Sloane could do was ask around among the

Opposite page: Spectators filled the seats at the first modern Olympics.

young men he knew. Four students from the College of New Jersey at Princeton were interested.

Then Sloane asked his former research assistant, John Graham, to help. Graham coached football at Harvard University and knew some athletes from the Boston Athletic Association who might like to join the team. He found eight men with various skills, from running to shooting.

Another Boston-area athlete also was interested. He was James B. Connolly, who wanted to enter both high- and long-jumping contests. He was a student at Harvard, and because the Games interfered with classes, he asked for a leave of absence to train and to go to Greece. Harvard turned him down. Determined to compete, Connolly dropped out of the university; even after the Olympics, he never tried to return.

America's first Olympians trained together over the summer of 1895 and kept in condition on their own until March of 1896.

Some team members were wealthy enough to pay their own way to Greece, but most needed financial help. Sloane tried to raise money to send the team abroad. At the last moment, Oliver Ames—a former governor of Massachusetts—helped find the money for all but two tickets.

Dr. Sloane and his wife, who had saved all year to pay their own passage,[35] did what had to be done. They handed their tickets to the last two athletes, and Dr. Sloane, vice president of the IOC, sat out the Games in New Jersey, where he combed the newspapers for rare reports of events in Athens. Also, the team coach, John Graham, sent him a daily telegram about the events taking place.[36] The telegrams were one way the team could show its appreciation for Sloane's selfless action.

The 13-man team and its coach sailed on March 21, 1896, aboard the SS *Fulda*. They exercised daily on the afterdeck and developed "sea legs"— the ability to move with the rhythm of a ship. Sea legs, however, don't work well on land; once the athletes landed, they would have to get their "land legs" back, and they would have to do it fast. The Games would begin the day after the Americans were scheduled to arrive in Athens.

The *Fulda* docked in Naples, on the western coast of Italy, and the team boarded a train to Brindisi— on the other side of the Italian peninsula. Another boat took them from Brindisi to Patras, Greece, and then a train brought them into Athens. They were exhausted by the travel, but there was no time to rest. After being greeted with bands and banners, they marched through the streets to their hotel, which seemed miles from the station.

At the hotel, they were welcomed by long speeches—all in Greek, of course—and offered heavy wine to drink. The Americans knew it would be rude to refuse the wine, so they drank, but they wondered whether this was a plot to weaken them for the next day's contests.

April 6, 1896, was a cloudy day, but that didn't stop huge crowds from pouring into the Panathenaic Stadium. Three hundred athletes waited on the

"This Marvelous Result"

Spectators await the opening ceremonies for the 1896 Games.

Coubertin's Olympics

The start of the 100-meter dash. The runner with both hands on the ground is Thomas Burke from the United States, using a starting technique generally unfamiliar to sprinters from other countries.

field, and at 3 P.M., King George—flanked by Queen Olga, their sons and daughters, and visiting royalty from Austria and Serbia—said the words that initiated the Games: "I hereby proclaim the opening of the First International Olympic Games in Athens." Cannons roared, and a flock of doves was released.

Two things became obvious almost at the start. First, in addition to being the wrong shape, the surface of the track was not good for running. It was a cinder track, and the cinders, sharp little pieces of hard charcoal, should have been mixed with clay. Instead they were loose, which made footing unsure, falls painful, and wounds dirty.

The second obvious thing was that the American athletes were going to be the ones to beat in the track events. The Americans had fielded no fencers, rope climbers, or cyclists, but they could run, jump, and throw.

The Europeans had never seen runners crouch at the start of a race to "take their marks" the way the Americans did. The crouch, and the push they got from their leading leg, gave the American runners an initial burst of speed that made them hard to beat. An American won each of the first three trials (pre-championship races) of the 100-meter dash, even though the Americans were used to running counter-clockwise and the Olympic courses were run clockwise.

Loud cheers from the stands made the Europeans

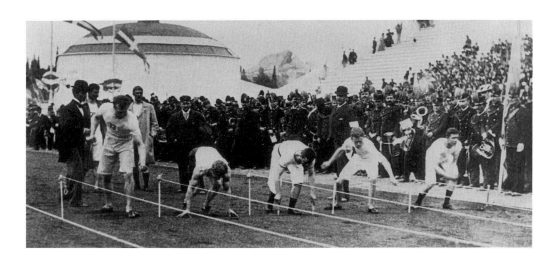

turn to see who was so noisy. It was a group of sailors from the U.S. warship *San Francisco*, joined by some students from American University in Athens. Just as if they were in a football stadium back home, they shouted war whoops and locomotive cheers, "rah-rah" chants that gained speed like an accelerating train. They did this for every excellent performance, whether the athlete was American or not. The Greeks quickly caught on and joined in.

The first championship event on the first day was called the "hop, skip, and jump"—what is now called the triple jump. Renegade Harvard student James Connolly made a flamboyant gesture. His turn came after the French competitor had a healthy lead in the contest. Before he jumped, Connolly tossed his cap about a yard past the Frenchman's mark. The crowd was shocked by his audacity, but when he landed beyond his cap, Connolly received wild cheers. He was the first athlete in more than 1,500 years to win in Olympic competition.

Many writers tell of how the U.S. team "swept" the first Olympics. This is true only of the track-and-field events, where Americans won 9 out of 12 events; they lost the 3 longest races. The Germans and the Greeks won the gymnastics and wrestling prizes, respectively; French cyclists and fencers took honors. Hungarians and Austrians beat the field in swimming events; Britons and Danes led in weightlifting.

One of the more surprising contests of the first Games was the discus throw. The Greeks were sure they would win, since throwing this flat metal weight was one of their traditional sports. The Americans tended to agree with them. They had a discus thrower, a student from Princeton named Robert Garrett, but his few months of training could not match the Greeks' years of practice. Garrett had gotten someone to make a discus like one he'd seen in a drawing of an ancient Olympic contest. It was heavy and awkward, but he had grown used to it.

In Athens, Garrett saw a real discus for the first time. A friendly Greek competitor lent him one, thinking the American would throw poorly since he hadn't practiced with the proper equipment. The

James Connolly

The classic discus stance is shown in the statue Discobolus. *Robert Garrett's stance was noticeably different, especially in the position of his feet and his non-throwing arm.*

disk was lighter and more streamlined than Garrett's. At that point, Garrett may have suspected that his practice with the heavier disk would make throwing the lighter one a lot easier.

But Garrett still wondered whether he should even bother to enter the contest against the Greek experts. Then he happened to see Professor Sloane's friend—the Frenchman with the big moustache. What was his name? Oh, yes, Monsieur de Coubertin. Garrett decided to ask for advice. In his precise English, Coubertin assured Garrett he should enter the event and give it his best.

The Greeks had style. They began their throws in a classic stance, like that in the famous statue *Discobolus* ("The Discus Thrower") by the sculptor Myron. In releasing the discus, the Greeks threw with a beautifully straight arm. Garrett, in contrast, crouched at the beginning of the throw and spun around to follow thróugh. He beat the best Greek throw by seven inches (18 centimeters).

As the days passed and more champions were hailed, it seemed that all Greece was aglow with Olympic fervor. The American athletes were especially popular, and they were entertained wherever they went. By the last day, when the Greek shepherd Spiridon Loues won the marathon race, it was hard to convince spectators that American victories belonged to America and not to Greece. All the athletes seemed to be Greek during that festive season.

The only American who was not exactly a star of the Games was a swimmer, Gardner Williams, who was accustomed to swimming in indoor pools. After he dove into the icy Bay of Zea to swim the 100 meters, Williams came up yelling, "I'm freezing!" and hauled himself back onto the pier.

On the final Sunday of the Games, which ran 10 days, the king of Greece invited 250 people to a breakfast banquet. He graciously included one M. le Baron Pierre de Coubertin on the list of guests, but not on the list of speakers.

In his own speech, the king thanked "all those who have worked to secure this marvelous result." First he thanked his sons, Nicholas, Constantine, and

George. Then he thanked George Averoff who had donated the money to restore the stadium. He thanked the Athenian organizers who had worked closely with the princes; he thanked all the athletes who had competed.

He did not mention his countryman, IOC president Demetrios Bikelas. Nor did he mention Pierre de Coubertin.

Spiridon Loues poses with other participants in the Athens Olympics.

8

THE LUSTER TARNISHED

At the breakfast banquet at the end of the first modern Olympics, King George of Greece announced that he wanted all future Olympic Games to be held in Athens. Many people agreed with him. Members of the U.S. Olympic team signed a petition in support of a Greek site for all the Games. This support was one way of thanking the Greeks for their friendship.

Pierre de Coubertin once again felt his grand scheme under attack. He firmly believed that every major city in the world should have a chance to stage Olympic Games. If they were always in Athens, they would never be more than a local Greek festival. His dream of international sport would slowly die.

Also, unless the Games stayed international, there would never be a Paris Olympics. At the Sorbonne congress in 1894, Paris had been selected to host the second Olympics, to be held at the same time as the 1900 Paris World's Fair. A successful Paris Olympics would be Coubertin's way of saying to France, "I was not such a fool after all."

Opposite page: The high jump competition during the 1900 Games. Rather than watching from stadium seats, spectators crane their necks for a good view from behind a fence.

73

King George presents prizes at the end of the first set of Games.

But the Greeks could not be stopped. The Games were now closely associated with Greece in the minds of all who followed sport in the press. "Greek Olympics" had wide support—even though Greece had problems with poor transportation, a fragile economy, and political instability. If there were to be Paris Games in 1900, they would have to compete with the Olympics that the Greeks were determined to have that year.[37]

On the Wednesday after the last of the Games, at an award ceremony in the stadium, King George presented a silver medal and an olive branch cut from a tree at Olympia to the first-place winners in each event. Second-place winners received bronze medals and laurel branches. Certificates of participation also were awarded, as were some special cups and trophies that had been donated by individuals or groups. Coubertin attended the award ceremony, but it was one more chance for the Greeks to ignore him.

After the first Olympic Games were over, Pierre took his bride to the Greek island of Corfu for a vacation that would be the honeymoon they had missed.

Marie was annoyed by the way the Greeks had ignored Pierre. She felt her husband should have been the hero of the Games—praised and rewarded, not shoved aside and neglected. She urged him to claim recognition for his great accomplishment. Pierre pointed to groups of Greek children playing "Olympic Games" in the fields of Corfu. He told her this was reward enough for him.

Pierre was putting on an act for Marie's sake, to take the edge off her anger. As some of his later writings would show, in his heart he was deeply hurt by the way he'd been cheated of credit for his creation.

On Corfu, Marie found out she was going to have a baby. In those days, a pregnant French woman spent as little time as possible in public, even if the birth were eight or nine months away. The couple hurried back to Paris.

Coubertin decided to behave as though the Greeks and their Olympic plans did not exist and to make sure that the 1900 Games would go on as planned in Paris. He began the difficult task of negotiating with city officials. He knew that Parisians didn't care about athletic contests. Still, the success of the Greek Olympics, which had received some coverage in the French press, might make Paris willing, if not eager, to be the Olympics' second city. Even before he left for Athens, he had started plans for a Paris Olympics. Now he refined those plans and turned them over to the organizers of the Paris World's Fair, who in turn gave the plans to bureaucrats in the Ministry of Public Instruction.

Coubertin's plan called for an Olympic zone, dedicated to athletics, separate from the fair. The employees at the ministry didn't understand or care what Olympics meant. They ignorantly mauled Pierre's plan and chopped up the Olympics. Gymnastics events were put with the fair's children's games. Rowing and yacht races were to join an exhibit of ocean-going cargo ships. Fencing matches were to be held next to a display of knives and forks.

Pierre was so busy arguing with the ministry that the birth of his first child, Jacques, late in 1896, made for only a pleasant interruption in his work.

But he was pleased that the baby was healthy and that his son would carry on the name of Coubertin. Pierre also hoped that his own father, who had been so unhappy with Pierre's choices of a career and a bride, might be pleased and proud of him at last for giving him a grandson.

A meeting of the International Olympic Committee was to be held in 1897. By this time, the plans for a 1900 Greek Olympics were dead—killed by a war between Greece and Turkey. Weakened by war, Greece could not organize another Olympics in the near future. The IOC's original plans for a 1900 Paris Olympics could proceed. So could its plan for Pierre de Coubertin to be the IOC's second president.

Coubertin didn't dare let the IOC members know how badly Olympic preparations were going in Paris. He arranged to hold the 1897 meeting in Le Havre, in northern France. In his invitations to the members, he wrote that a Paris meeting would be too dangerous because Parisians were upset and angry over the trial of a supposed spy named Dreyfus. At the meeting, to avoid revealing that the Paris Olympics might be a disaster, he steered discussion away from the upcoming Games. Instead, he had the group go over the Athens Games to see where mistakes had been made and how they could be avoided in the future. Coubertin established a tradition with this ploy; even a century later, the IOC still reviews all the events of the previous Games in preparation for the future.

The IOC does not get involved with the details of an Olympic meet. They don't figure out where athletes will sleep, or who will print tickets, or what the opening ceremony should be like. Those decisions belong to an Olympic Organizing Committee formed by the host city. In Paris, the Ministry of Public Instruction was acting as the OOC—and doing a terrible job.

After the IOC meeting, Coubertin went back to work on the Paris Games. Without telling the Ministry of Public Instruction, he formed a new OOC filled with his young, aristocratic friends. Because the Athens Games had been so successful, these men pledged their own money to repeat the success in Paris. They began planning a set of Games according to Coubertin's dreams and plans. One gentleman, Robert Fournier-Sarlovèze, volunteered to head the OOC. He was associated with a club whose several fine playing fields could be used for track events. Eighteen committee members agreed to be stewards—that is, they took over planning all meets and events for a given sport. Other venues were added for cycling, horseback events, boxing, and water polo.

Then, much to the baron's surprise, the Union of French Athletic Sports Clubs—which he had founded—declared itself to be the only legitimate OOC for the 1900 Games. Union members would not cooperate with Coubertin's rich friends. This declaration may have started as a way to gain some positions of power on the existing OOC, but it greatly disturbed Pierre's committee of aristocrats. The wealthy gentlemen—who, after all, were risking their own money—did not care to play by the rules of others. They walked away.

Coubertin didn't care who the OOC was, as long as the Games were successful. But when he saw that the union's OOC list contained the names of almost every active politician in France, he smelled trouble. To protect his reputation as an independent, non-political IOC president, he could not associate too closely with the union's efforts. He had to work only unofficially, helping with matters that were not in the OOC's domain. His first action was to tour Europe, inviting teams to participate in the 1900 Games. He also tried to establish permanent National Olympic Committees (NOCs) in each country, so there would be some way to select participants through official channels.

Then tragedy called Pierre home. His baby, Jacques, left in the sun too long, suffered a heatstroke. The baby did not die, but his brain was badly damaged. As he grew, he never mastered more than the basic skills of life, and independence, education, and career were forever out of his reach. Marie, perhaps out of her deep sorrow, became angry at everyone around

Coubertin didn't care who the OOC was, as long as the Games were successful.

her, including her husband. Psychology was in its infancy at the time, and Marie had no tools for putting her world back together. All she could do was make others suffer with her, and this she did very well, for the rest of Pierre's life.

Pierre coped with the tragedy by keeping himself busier than ever with the business of the IOC—and with his writing. Over the next few years, he wrote a short history called *France depuis 1814* ("France since 1814"), and he started a longer, seven-volume history of France called *La Chronique de France* ("The History of France"). He also wrote a wildly romantic novel about his own childhood and youth, called *Le Roman d'un rallié* ("Memories of a Convert"). The histories did not establish him as a historian; the novel did not establish him as a novelist.

Meanwhile, the 1900 Games were turning into a huge failure. One of the biggest mistakes involved scheduling. Instead of holding events every day for two or three weeks, the OOC arranged a meet every now and then from July through October. The official program didn't even contain the word "Olympics." Attendance was poor, and French judges refused to be impartial. Many athletes thought they were running a preliminary race or giving a demonstration, when they were actually in an official Olympic event.

There was no track at all, only some stakes marking a course across a grassy field full of hills and bumps. In throwing contests such as the discus and the shot put, the equipment frequently landed in a clump of trees, and the throws couldn't be measured.

Thirty-five Americans—many of them college students from Princeton, the University of Pennsylvania, and Syracuse University—went to France to compete. They amazed their hosts by refusing (at their coaches' urging) to attend any ceremonies or competitions on Sundays, which they considered holy. They won 17 of the 22 track-and-field events.

A few changes adopted by the IOC for the Paris Olympics became permanent features of the Games. One was the addition of events for team sports. Coubertin opposed this vigorously; in his eyes the

Team sports, such as tug-of-war and soccer, made their first appearances at the 1900 Olympics.

Olympics were to show how the individual could excel. The IOC outvoted its president and allowed soccer, team rowing, and relay footraces—as well as cricket, croquet, and tug-of-war.

Another change that horrified Coubertin was that women were allowed to compete, if only in tennis and golf. If he had his choice, Coubertin would never have allowed it. Women, in his opinion, should attend the Games, provide applause, and stay off the playing field.

The Paris Olympics were a bitter disappointment to Coubertin. None of his plans had been followed, none of his dreams had come true.

Women in the Olympics

Women in ancient Greece could compete in many competitions, including the Pythian, Isthmian, Herean, Asclepian, and Sicyonian Games. But they were barred from the Olympic Games. In the 1,200-year known history of the ancient Olympics, women were not even allowed at the site. The penalty for breaking this taboo was death.

As he planned to revive the Olympics in the late 19th century, Pierre de Coubertin could not have been unaware that women enjoyed sports. All around him, women were playing croquet, tennis, and golf. They rode bicycles, rowed boats, and even fenced. But since he believed that women didn't belong in sporting arenas, Pierre tried to exclude them from competing in the Olympics. Finally, they clamored so loudly that he could not keep them out.

One woman actually applied to the Athens Organizing Committee as a candidate for the marathon in 1896. Her name was Melpomene (Mel-*pom*-un-nee). When she was refused entry as a competitor, she decided to run anyway. She ran alongside the road the men took, so she often had no decent running surface. Even so, she finished the race only 1½ hours slower than Spiridon Loues, the winner.

For the Paris Olympics of 1900, two women's sporting events were listed as part of the Games: golf and tennis. This was most likely done without Coubertin's knowledge or

Florence Griffith-Joyner's race clothes would have shocked Pierre.

This time, he hadn't just been ignored. He had given a wonderful gift to the city and country he loved, and the French—including his fellow sports lovers in the athletic union—had trampled on it. His feelings of personal rejection had to be profound.

The question of why the baron hadn't taken a more active role in Paris remains. He knew the members of the athletic union; he probably knew most of the politicians. He knew how to use tact and diplomacy, how to wine and dine the right people, and how the Games should be played. Perhaps

consent. The two events were unofficial, meaning they would not be recorded in the official Olympic annuals. Nevertheless, the events established a precedent for allowing women to compete in the Olympics. Men could never again say the Games were strictly for male athletes.

Women competed in archery and tennis—again unofficially—at the St. Louis Games of 1904. Four years later, the London OOC found ice-skating facilities for a summer event for women, and instituted a yachting event for them. This was the first set of Games where women were recognized as official competitors. In 1912, Stockholm organizers put swimming and diving on the program for women.

Eventually, women began organizing themselves into sporting federations and holding their own competitions. One of the most able organizers was Alice Milliat of France. Milliat founded the Fédération Sportive Féminine Internationale, and it was she who finally succeeded in pressuring the IOC to include women in major Olympic sports.

Milliat's group had organized a set of women's games to be held every four years, with the first competition taking place in Paris in 1922 and drawing 20,000 spectators. The success of the women's competitions and pressure from women's sports groups forced the IOC to add major sports for women. In addition to swimming, diving, and fencing at the 1928 Olympics in Amsterdam, women competed in team gymnastics and track and field at the Olympics. From then on, women's participation in the Games rose.

Most Olympic events are still same-sex—that is, women don't compete with men. Of all the women's sports, ice skating and gymnastics draw the most attention. Maybe that's because people still like to see grace and style from women rather than strength and speed. But in the late 20th century we are seeing nearly equal interest in men's and women's events in track, swimming, and tennis.

he was overwhelmed by his personal problems; perhaps when he saw what the union planned, he stopped caring.

Pierre had foreseen the ruin of the Paris Games, so perhaps he took comfort in the fact that he had removed himself from the Paris OOC. But the luster the Olympics had gained in Athens had been tarnished by Parisian mismanagement.

Despite the Paris fiasco, the Olympics had caught the spark of life. No one was talking about abandoning future Games.

9

THE GAMES REBOUND

The IOC intended the 1904 Games to be held in the United States, but which American city would act as host? Even after the chaos of the Paris Games, IOC members still thought combining Olympics with world's fairs was a good idea. The IOC expected to get a proposal from St. Louis, scheduled to hold a 1904 world's fair. When this didn't happen by their 1901 meeting in Paris, they awarded the Games to Chicago.

At that same meeting, as expected, Coubertin nominated Professor William Milligan Sloane, the IOC member in the United States, to be president for the four years until the Games. But Sloane understood that the IOC must be free from the influence of any government. In matters related to the Olympics, the IOC president should not owe loyalty to any group but the IOC. It would be better, he believed, for the president to be from outside the host country. Therefore, he nominated Coubertin as president for life. The members heartily supported the idea.

But the baron refused. He said he could not accept

Opposite page: Melvin Sheppard of the United States, with Harold Wilson of Great Britain on his heels, wins the 1,500-meter run at the 1908 Olympics in London. These Games were a huge success.

that much power. Instead, he agreed to serve as president for a 10-year term. Once again Pierre renounced what he seemed to want. When power and recognition were offered, he turned away with a humble gesture.

Then again, all this might have been a show of courtesy between two friends. Sloane was not hungry for more honors or titles. He already had a profession and a good reputation as a scholar. Reviving the Olympics was the work to which Coubertin had dedicated his life. Sloane, a good friend of Pierre's, may have sensed that the baron didn't want to give up the title or the power.[38]

The IOC adopted the baron's idea to create International Federations (IFs)—organizations to make rules and set standards—for every sport. For instance, the Fédération Internationale de Gymnastique makes all the rules for performing and judging gymnastic events. Coubertin backed these IFs because they kept the IOC out of arguments over rules.

Coubertin was cooking up an alphabet soup of organizations. The IOC delegated the OOCs to work through the NOCs to get AAU (Amateur Athletic Union) members to play by IF rules.

With so many people involved at so many levels, Coubertin finally had all the support he needed. Now, instead of lists of the wealthy and titled, his Olympic Committee stationery featured names of people who were really interested in international sports. After nearly 20 years of hard work, Pierre could relax a little and try to build a normal life with his family.

In May of 1902, Pierre and Marie had a baby girl whom they named Renée. She grew into a sunny, bright little girl who pleased her father with her pretty paintings and poems.

*Pierre and Marie's
daughter, Renée*

In addition to Renée and the five-year-old, infant-like Jacques, Pierre and Marie took pride in their nephews Guy and Bernard, the sons of Pierre's eldest brother, Paul. Pierre also enjoyed a close friendship with another of his nephews, Maurice de Madre, the son of Pierre's sister, Marie. Although younger than Pierre, Maurice was one of Pierre's "best-loved companions."[39]

About this time, Greece was recovering from its war with Turkey and asked to have the Olympics restored to Athens. The IOC was not in a good bargaining position. Athens had been a success, Paris a failure. But the committee wanted to continue with its international program. In 1904, a compromise was reached: Greece would host "interim Games" every four years, two years after each Olympics.

Plans for a Chicago Olympics were proceeding when word came from St. Louis that the organizers of the fair were determined to have athletic competitions. If they weren't Olympics, they would be "championships."

Chicago organizers predicted failure if the two meets competed for the best athletic talent. They knew most tourists would go to St. Louis, where they could get both a world's fair and sports—twice the entertainment for their money. The IOC bowed to pressure and transferred the Games to St. Louis.

The Hall of Festivals at the 1904 World's Fair in St. Louis

President Theodore Roosevelt, honorary chairman of the 1904 Games, may have been among those applying pressure to change locations.

It was an unfortunate decision. The Games required an identity of their own. As the Paris Games showed, the excitement of the Games was dulled if they were combined with another event. The Olympics needed a crowd who came to see athletics, not just fairgoers who happened to see a footrace on their way to the farm-machinery exhibit.

The decision was made, however, for a set of Olympic Games in St. Louis. The St. Louis OOC felt that the Games and the fair should be of equal length, that is, from May to November. To fill so many months with competitions, the OOC accepted as an Olympic event almost any vaguely athletic meet. The committee announced 38 contests, including roque (a game similar to croquet) and tobacco-juice spitting.

Baron de Coubertin decided he would not attend. Seven months was too long to live away from his family. And perhaps, since his only income came

Coubertin's family: Pierre, Renée, Marie, Jacques, and "Madame"—Marie's mother

from his family money, the baron was facing financial problems. Many other Europeans also chose to skip these drawn-out American Games; only two European members of the IOC attended. Very few non-American athletes competed.

The baron read reports of the Games in the Parisian newspapers, in the comfort of his home. He was heartened to learn that the Games received so much press attention, but he seems not to have regretted his decision to stay home. He was especially glad he did not see "Anthropology Days," a bizarre set of contests among Native Americans, indigenous peoples of other countries, and even some "freaks" from a carnival. Many of the contestants in these cruel events couldn't understand English and didn't know the rules of the games they were playing. The "fun" for the spectators lay in ridiculing the players. Coubertin wrote, "In no place but America would one have dared to place such events on a program...but to Americans everything is permissible."[40] This was not meant as a compliment. Coubertin had always considered sport a gentlemen's pastime. Mocking innocent people did not fit that description.

During the years after the Paris Olympics, Pierre turned once again to his writing. His seven-volume history, *La Chronique de France*, was published between 1900 and 1906, and he wrote many articles, essays, and short books about sports and about the Olympics. They went by such titles as "National Strength and Sports" and "Useful Gymnastics."

He had not stopped hoping that sports would reform education, a hope reflected in some of his articles—for example, "Are the Public Schools a Failure? A French View." He also wrote articles on how to make the Olympics better, more spectacular, and easier to manage. And he wrote about his Olympic experiences.

Many of Coubertin's articles and essays try to define "Olympism," the name he gave to the movement he'd founded. In trying to explain Olympism, he used three themes: religion, peace, and beauty.

The Olympics were a *religion* for Coubertin. Just

like other religions, it had a central ideal principle—the celebration of the soul through sport. Where religions had rites, the Olympics had ceremonies. Where religions had credos, traditions, and observances, the Olympics had rules, contests, and celebrations. Of course, Pierre felt that he was the high priest of Olympism.

As to *peace*, Pierre hoped international competitions would help the world reach a golden age in which there would be no war and no conflict. The Olympics, like many other international meetings, had peace and understanding as its goal. Coubertin had faith that sportsmanship was the answer.

Beauty was the third side of Olympism. Coubertin wrote about the grace and form of the athletes, the pageantry of the opening and closing ceremonies, and the solemn rites for winners, with bouquets, anthems, and medals.

The baron had always hoped to find a way to incorporate more art into the Games, and at a 1905 meeting in Brussels attended by the IOC and leaders of sporting federations, the idea was considered. Contests in architecture, painting, sculpture, literature, and music were to be part of future Games.

At this conference, the IOC made several other important decisions. They awarded the 1908 Games to Rome, Italy. And they decided to publish a bulletin, *The Olympic Review,* to keep members in touch with IOC activities between meetings. This productive conference was handled by the Belgian member, Count Henri de Baillet-Latour, an expert organizer who would be important to the future of the IOC.

In 1906, Panhellenic Games were held for the first time, fulfilling the agreement made between the IOC and Greece in 1904. Even though Panhellenic means "related to all of Greece," the contestants were not just from Greece but from several nations, and the games had an international feel. These games gave a boost to the Olympic spirit, and a boost was sorely needed. The Paris Games had not been satisfactory, and the St. Louis Games had not been attended by very many Europeans. Europeans were hungry to see first-rate competition. At the Panhellenic Games,

Greece staged another great success. Even the royal family of Great Britain attended.

By 1907, Pierre had accumulated a huge archive of Olympic materials. As a historian, he was aware that future researchers would be grateful for any scrap of paper connected with the Games, and he kept everything. The IOC charter stated that all these papers should be sent to the OOC of the current Olympiad, but in reality, they had never left the baron's home in Paris.

These papers needed a home of their own.

The Panhellenic Games were held in the same stadium as the 1896 Olympics.

The Swiss member of the IOC, Colonel de Loys, suggested that Pierre choose a site in Switzerland. Because of Switzerland's national policy of neutrality —of not entering wars or taking sides in international conflicts—it could offer a relatively safe home for the Olympic archives. Loys hosted the baron on a journey around the beautiful alpine country, and Coubertin was impressed. He visited several more times on his own, thinking about where and when to relocate his collection.

The plans made by Rome to hold the next Games collapsed when Mt. Vesuvius, a volcano near Naples, erupted in 1906. The cost of rebuilding put too great a strain on the Italian government, and the organizers had to tell the IOC to make new arrangements.

Great Britain stepped in; London would gladly host the 1908 Games. The head of London's OOC, W. H. Grenfell, Lord Desborough, was determined that the Games "should be organised and celebrated in a fashion worthy of this country's sporting fame."[41] He accomplished this by following the many instructions, plans, and guidelines Baron de Coubertin had written over the years. The 1908 Olympics were a great success in the manner of Athens—a real festival of sport.

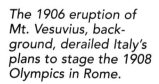

The 1906 eruption of Mt. Vesuvius, background, derailed Italy's plans to stage the 1908 Olympics in Rome.

Even so, the London Games were marred by what many considered unfair judging, which was especially pro-British and anti-American. For example, the British were sure their man could win in the 400-meter run, but they feared the Americans. British judges stood at 20-yard intervals around the track to catch any technical errors the Americans might make. The judges thought American J. C. Carpenter "ran wide," running into a lane reserved for Britain's Wyndham Halswelle and blocking him when he tried to pass. Lanes had not been marked out for this race, and there was no physical contact between the runners, but the judges cried foul anyway, broke the winner's tape, and voided the race. Carpenter was disqualified from the rematch, for which strings were laid out to mark the lanes. The other two Americans withdrew from the event in protest.

When another American, Mel Sheppard, won the 1500-meter race, the British headline read: "Why Wilson Didn't Win," and Sheppard was hardly mentioned. In the tug-of-war, the British team members were allowed to wear boots with steel rims because those were "everyday footwear." After one try, the U.S. team quit in disgust.

Race officials break the tape ahead of would-be winner J. C. Carpenter at the end of the 400-meter run.

Coubertin's Olympics

Right: Officials appear to be helping marathon runner Dorando Pietri stay on his feet near the finish line of the 1908 marathon Below: After the race, Pietri is whisked away on a stretcher.

This Olympic meet became famous because of a sad event at the end of the marathon. An Italian runner named Dorando Pietri was first to run into the stadium for the final lap of the race. He had not paced himself well during the cross-country part of the race, and he was exhausted and disoriented. He started to run the wrong way around the track. Officials rushed to help him. They turned him around, supported him, and dragged him across the finish line, where he collapsed. When he came to, he found he had been disqualified for receiving help in running the race. But Queen Alexandra of England gave him a personal gift of a large, gold trophy as a consolation.

Afterwards, Pietri said,

> I was all right until I entered the stadium. When I heard the people cheering and knew I had nearly won, a thrill passed through me and I felt my strength going. I fell down, but tried to struggle to the tape, but fell again. I never lost consciousness of what was going on, and if the doctor had not ordered the attendants to pick me up, I believe I could have finished unaided.[42]

Since Pietri nearly died the afternoon of the race, he was probably wrong about being able to finish.

In retrospect, Coubertin looked at the conflicts of the 1908 Games as valuable. He wrote that "these sudden bursts of violence seem to have given [the Games] added interest."[43]

Pietri with the Queen's Cup

10

Honor at Stockholm

Four years later, Stockholm, Sweden, offered a well-run, exciting set of Games. But before this could be accomplished, many political problems had to be overcome. The International Federations for rowing and cycling threatened to withdraw because their members felt Greece was the only proper place for the Games. But after the 1906 Panhellenic Games, Greece withdrew from the Olympic arena until its unsuccessful bid for the 100th anniversary Games.

Also, in these years just before World War I, some countries claimed to own others. For instance, Russia claimed Finland, and Austria wanted Hungary to march under the Austrian flag. And there was the problem of fair judging. No one wanted a repeat of the problems in London.

All these difficulties brought the Stockholm Games close to disaster. But the baron, Professor Sloane, and other IOC members—by tact, delaying, cajoling, flattering, and assuring—were able to keep the 1912 Games alive.

Opposite page: Pierre in his office

The team from the United States traveled to Sweden on an ocean liner that docked at the port of Stockholm. Then the athletes used the ship as a hotel and a training center. A running track was set up on the deck. Throwers attached ropes to their javelins and discuses and then hauled them back from the sea after each practice throw.

Equestrian (horseback) events were introduced during this Olympiad, even though the baron thought it was unfair that riders couldn't compete unless they owned their own horse and could pay to ship it to Stockholm.

Some female swimmers and divers were registered for the 1912 Games—probably over Coubertin's objections. He did not approve of women putting themselves at risk in sports. When women started to fly planes, he was horrified at their participation in air shows. He wrote,

> It is indecent that the spectators should be exposed to the risk of seeing the body of a woman being smashed before their very eyes. Besides, no matter how toughened a sportswoman may be, her organism is not cut out to sustain certain shocks.[44]

Coubertin was so shocked by the female flyers that he proposed rules to prevent them from flying in air show competitions. Later, regarding more conventional sports, he advocated separate Olympic Games for women,[45] supposedly to give the public a chance to decide if women's sports were worth watching. Later, the baron claimed that the only reason spectators would watch women's sports would be to see their bodies exposed. Women's competition should be held in private if at all![46]

The Stockholm Games lasted five weeks. The streets were decked with flowers, and there were fireworks each night, despite the lack of real darkness at that time of year in Sweden. The stadium could be used as a banquet hall or a concert hall, and even on occasion, a ballroom. The Swedish OOC, led by Crown Prince Gustav Adolph, was

genial, thorough, efficient, and fair—though their insistence on using Swedish as the official language kept most foreigners from understanding many of the announcements.

The Stockholm OOC

Stockholm presented the first Olympic Art Festival. This event had been approved at one of Coubertin's lavish banquets for Olympic supporters in Paris in 1906. After the usual speeches, the conference agreed to Olympic competitions in architecture, sculpture, painting, music, and literature. All entries had to be linked to sport. For instance, architecture prizes went to designs for gymnasiums and other sports facilities.

The first literature prize was awarded to a long poem called "Ode to Sport." Though its authors were listed as "Hohrod" and "Eschbach," the real author was Pierre de Coubertin.

The arts competition was discontinued after 1948. The IOC decided that visitors to the Games wanted to see performances by athletes, not by musicians and painters. But every host city since 1948 has made some effort to include the arts as part of the celebration. The cities themselves usually become works of art, as banners and Olympic symbols blossom everywhere.

The Stockholm Olympics also were famous for a

Coubertin's Olympics

disqualification. Jim Thorpe of the United States won both the pentathlon and the decathlon (a set of 10 track events) in a great show of speed and strength. A year later, someone discovered that Thorpe had once been paid a small sum for playing baseball, and he was stripped of all his medals and honors.

An obscure American pentathlete named Avery Brundage also competed at Stockholm. Years later, he would become president of the IOC. Coubertin himself appeared and was honored in Stockholm. He enjoyed the Games from his seat in the royal box, next to King Gustav and his son.

War threatened Europe after the 1912 Olympics, and the IOC feared the 1916 Games would be played next to European battlefields. Coubertin wouldn't believe war was possible; he had worked too hard to bring about international understanding and peace.

To remind nations they were interdependently linked on the planet, he designed a symbol for the Olympics: five interlocked rings standing for the five parts of the world committed to participating in

Pierre hosted a lavish party for the IOC's 20th anniversary meeting.

the Games as of 1913 (North and South America, Europe, Africa, and Asia, in which Coubertin included Australia and New Zealand). Every nation in the world at that time could find the colors of its flag among the five colored rings (red, blue, yellow, green, and black) and the white background.

Coubertin's flag, with the rings above the motto *Citius, Altius, Fortius,* was not used at any Olympic Games until 1920. But it was first displayed in 1914, at a huge party Coubertin hosted for the IOC's 20th-anniversary meeting in Paris. This party was extravagant, even by the baron's standards. There were at least 17 receptions, as well as plays and operas, choral concerts, banquets, and a speech by the president of France.

At the IOC business meeting, the British delegates reminded the members that the chosen host for the 1916 Games was Berlin, Germany. This location, they said, might be unwise. Germany seemed to be looking for an excuse to start a war in Europe. But Coubertin had faith in the power of the Olympics to bring about world peace. He was sure that the spirit of Olympism would influence the German kaiser to keep peace in Europe. Many agreed with him, and Berlin was allowed to go on with its plans for the Games.

This time the baron was wrong. War came in 1914, and the 1916 Games were canceled. Coubertin's Olympic movement had not been able to prevent World War I. His Olympic ideals had no influence at all when nations struggled for power.

Well, if there was to be a war, Coubertin, a loyal Frenchman, would do his duty and fight for his country. He tried to enlist in the army, but the officers explained that he was too old to be a soldier. He was shocked and insulted. Too old? Why, he was only 51!

The Olympic flag

11

FROM THE ASHES OF WAR

World War I brought painful changes to Pierre de Coubertin's life. The German army threatened to attack Paris. The IOC offices—nothing more than rooms in Coubertin's home—could easily be bombed or burned. If that happened, all the records and resources for the Games would be lost.

And money was suddenly a problem for the baron. He had made some bad investments, and inflation eroded the value of his income. He was forced to put his family on a strict budget.

Marie de Coubertin was still an angry, bitter woman. She may have wanted more attention as the wife of the renovator of the Olympics, but Pierre would never allow her to play the role of "first lady." Now, without money, she could no longer play the role of an aristocrat.

Marie's family situation provided little solace. Not only was her son badly brain-damaged, but her daughter—a bright, lovely young woman—suffered bouts of mental illness. Every now and then, Renée de

Opposite page: Troops travel through war ruins en route to Verdun, France, during World War I.

The Coubertins on a picnic: Renée, Pierre, and Marie

Coubertin had to stay in a hospital until her mind cleared. Renée's care was another drain on the Coubertins' financial resources.

Marie, consumed by bitterness, did not always act rationally. For example, she often made her daughter wear boys' clothing. In the early 1900s, respectable French women didn't wear pants of any kind.

Pierre decided that because of the war, his lack of money, and the fragile mental health of his family, the time was right to move to Switzerland. A special IOC subcommittee was set up in 1912 to prepare new quarters for IOC operations. In April of 1915, papers were signed in the town hall of Lausanne, a Swiss city on the shores of Lake Geneva, making it the official home of the IOC.

By 1918, the Coubertin apartment on the rue Oudinot, where Pierre had been born, was sold. The chateau at Mirville had been sold many years earlier.

The baron's family moved into a simple hotel called Beau Séjour, made available to them by the city of Lausanne. They still had some money, but they had to live more frugally than ever before. They kept up the appearance of a well-to-do family, and the baron still traveled in Europe and took his family to the South of France in winter and to Normandy in the summer. But the days of hosting huge banquets for hundreds of people were over. Coubertin didn't even have an office for the IOC; business was done in his Lausanne hotel suite.

The baron became deeply depressed during the years of the First World War. His nephews Guy and Bernard, who were like sons to him, were killed in battle. Every bit of war news reminded him that his Games and his philosophy of Olympism had not prevented this conflict. He felt that he had wasted his life, and he considered resigning from the IOC. Once again he turned to writing to share his thoughts and feelings with a world too busy to care. He wrote steadily, turning out essays, biographies, and philosophical books.

As the war dragged to an end, people started talking about another set of Olympics. Word reached Pierre that his dream was very much alive. His spirits lifted, and he took up the challenge of holding Olympic Games in a shattered Europe.

In April of 1919, he called an IOC meeting. The committee decided it was important for the Games to be played on schedule, and they asked Antwerp, Belgium, to host the 1920 Games. Belgium was a victim of the war—the German army had invaded it in 1914—and the IOC wanted to honor the gallantry of the little nation. Antwerp was in ruins, but somehow a Belgian Olympic Organizing Committee got together the bare essentials for the Games. There was no money to redecorate the stadium. Athletes had to sleep on children's cots in a schoolhouse, eight to a room. The five rings of the baron's flag were used as a theme for decorating the shattered town, and the flag itself was flown at the Games for the first time.

Since women had participated so bravely in the war, the IOC was pressured to include women, but Coubertin held to his principles. He offered a "Charter of Sport Reform" that would ban women's participation in any meet where men were competing. He called this kind of athletic mixing "promiscuity in sport."[47] The IOC as a whole, however, did not adopt his proposed charter, and women participated in a few events.

As the war dragged to an end, people started talking about another set of Olympics. Word reached Pierre that his dream was very much alive.

Paavo Nurmi

Belgians were so poor in 1920 that the price of a ticket to the Olympics—the equivalent of about 30 U.S. cents—was too high for most people. Seats for many events were empty, so the Belgian Organizing Committee gave free tickets to schoolchildren.

Despite Belgium's handicaps, Coubertin was thrilled with the success of the 1920 Games. The king of Belgium spoke with him respectfully, calling him the father of the Olympics. So did the new "king" of Olympic track, Paavo Nurmi of Finland, who was so fast he was called "the Flying Finn." Pierre was reminded of the 1912 Games, when he was honored by both the king of Sweden and Jim Thorpe, the athletic "king" of that year.

But Pierre was 57, tired, limited in funds, and weighed down with family problems. Perhaps it was time to retire.

These were difficult days. The IOC was under attack from many sides. Some influential French people were trying to hand the Games over to the infant League of Nations, a short-lived international organization similar to the United Nations. Also, the International Federations of some sports were talking about replacing the Games with their own international championships.

Coubertin had to create some unity among these 99 factions. In addition, he had one unrealized ambition: to make France admit that organized sport was a valuable asset to society. The 1900 Paris Olympics had been too badly organized and poorly received to make much of an impression on French society.

At the IOC meeting in Lausanne in 1921, which was attended by leaders of many IFs and NOCs, he announced he would retire from the IOC in 1925. He asked the IOC whether they could, as a special favor, hold the 1924 Games in Paris. Amsterdam, the Netherlands city originally scheduled to host the 1924 Games, graciously agreed to step aside.

No one could deny the baron's wish. He was the renovator—the central figure of the Olympic movement—and his position within the IOC commanded respect, if not homage. He himself called it "a masterly coup!" and gloated that he had forced the IOC to plan two Olympiads ahead. This way, the future was assured for eight more years.[48]

The city of Lausanne was now prouder than ever that it had acquired a treasure like Pierre de Coubertin and the IOC. In appreciation, the town gave the IOC a mansion called Mon Repose for a headquarters.

During the four years between the 1920 and 1924 Olympics, the IOC decided that athletes who played winter sports should have their own Games. Coubertin didn't know if he liked the idea. On one hand, people loved to watch winter sports, and the skaters and skiers deserved the chance to be Olympians. On the other hand, winter Games might draw attention away from the summer activities.

Scandinavian IOC members were afraid that winter Olympics would steal the audience from the Nordic Games, traditional in the northern countries. But they also knew that northerners were best at most, if not all, winter sports, and would probably walk off with all the Olympic prizes, at least for the first few years.

The first winter competition was held in Chamonix, France, in 1924. The IOC made these rules:

1. The winter meet was a prelude to the summer Games, not a separate event.
2. Winter Games should be held in the same country as summer Games of the same year.
3. Winter Games were not to be called Olympics.

But the winter Games at Chamonix in 1924 were so popular that the IOC declared they were Olympics after all. The IOC again broke its own rules in 1928, when the winter Games were played in Switzerland, and the summer Games in Holland. Coubertin, too, had finally embraced the idea of winter Olympics. He wrote, "Our Scandinavian colleagues have been won over to our point of view entirely, and this made me very happy, as I had always wished to see this winter extension duly approved and endorsed."[49]

Mon Repose

Opening ceremonies for the first winter Olympic Games, held in Chamonix, France

12

TRIUMPH IN PARIS

Would the 1924 summer Games in Paris be the Games the baron had dreamed of—or another chaotic failure?

Things got off to a rocky start. Members of the Paris Municipal Council fought over the location of the new stadium. Coubertin wanted the structure to be in the center of Paris, near the Military Academy. He thought the students' barracks at the academy could be used as quarters for the athletes.[50] But the matter was out of his hands: the Paris OOC and the city council fought on.

Coubertin worried about whether they would ever agree. He knew that Los Angeles hoped to become an Olympic city soon and was already building a stadium for the purpose. He made sure that if Paris could not end its squabbling in time to prepare for the Games, Los Angeles would be waiting to take over.

Finally, the president of France, Alexandre Millerand, stepped in. He had lent his name in support

Opposite page: Pierre had become quite distinguished looking as he grew older.

of Paris as host to the Games, and he didn't want to be associated with a failure. He urged the council to come to a decision, and they decided to hold the Games in Colombe, a suburb northwest of the city.

At last, Paris began to cooperate with one of Coubertin's projects. The city seemed to realize how much money and prestige could be earned by presenting a successful Olympics.

In 1924, France was very poor; Paris had no money in its treasury to donate toward the Games, and prices were sky-high. But the Paris OOC was determined to put on a great show. Somehow, the money was found. The river Seine, which runs through Paris, flooded in the summer of 1923. Work on the Games fell behind schedule. But by May of 1924, all was ready, and Coubertin watched his dream come true.

Once again, the American team used an ocean liner as a traveling gymnasium. In Colombe, the Americans stayed in a concrete barracks on an estate once owned by one of Napoleon's generals. The team officials stayed at the estate's chateau, one of the largest houses on the property. On their first night there, the athletes pitched in to fight a fire that burned many houses in a nearby village. Then they took up a collection to aid the family of the one villager who was killed. This endeared the team to the French public.

At the opening ceremonies, a content, very proud Pierre de Coubertin sat with England's Prince of Wales, the king of Romania, the ruler of Abyssinia (Ethiopia), and the new president of France, Gaston Domergue.

Some of the drama of these Games, as experienced by several track athletes, was re-created in an Academy Award-winning movie, *Chariots of Fire*. The movie didn't show that the temperature reached 113°F (about 45°C) in the stadium, or that the swimming and diving events were held in the muddy Seine, where the current ran strong.

And no movie star took the part of the French baron. He was not even mentioned.

The American swimming squad of 1924 was a

particularly notable group. One member, Gertrude Ederle, won three medals. Two years later, she swam the English Channel, making the swim almost two hours faster than the existing men's record. Johnny Weissmuller, another U.S. swimmer, was one of the brightest stars of the 1924 Games. He won three medals in one day—one for the 100-meter freestyle, one for a lap of the 200-meter relay, and one for water polo. Between events, he and a friend put on a comedy diving show to amuse the crowds.

Weissmuller gets the credit for making swimming a prominent Olympic sport. Before 1924, track-and-field events had overshadowed all other forms of Olympic sport. But the handsome swimmer made the world aware that water sports could be exciting for spectators. Weissmuller also became one of the first athletes to cash in on his Olympic fame. After his second Olympics, a Hollywood studio offered him a contract. He might not have been a great actor, but as Tarzan he made many popular movies. Weissmuller's fame, however, raised the question of whether athletes ought to use their Olympic medals as a launching pad for other public careers.

Though swimmers like Weissmuller could compete in a cool environment, runners were exposed to the unusual heat of Paris and had to cope with it. Runners from Finland once again made the world notice them. Paavo Nurmi, who had taken medals and earned fame four years earlier in Antwerp, again was a winner, taking four gold medals. His Finnish teammate Ville "Willie" Ritola ran a total of 39,000 meters in seven days—and won a medal in every event he entered. He never did beat Nurmi, though.

Nurmi was the only runner who did not seem affected by the ferocious heat during the 10-kilometer cross-country race. When he crossed the finish line, he was 500 meters ahead of the nearest competitor, Ritola. Then the crowd watched, horrified, as others staggered in, disoriented and exhausted. One ran the wrong way, if one could call his lurching gait a run. He fell, got up, turned the right way, and managed to make the circuit to the finish line. As the

Gertrude Ederle

Johnny Weissmuller

*Vincent Richards of the
United States won a
gold medal in the last
tennis events to be held
in the Olympics until
1988.*

crowd cheered, another runner entered the stadium, ran into a wall, and seriously injured himself.

At these Paris Games, tennis saw its last Olympics for 64 years. No longer attractive as an amateur competition, it was dropped as of the 1928 Games and not reinstated until 1988.

No statistics can describe what these Paris Games meant to Pierre de Coubertin. On the verge of retirement, he realized a lifelong dream: to see Olympics succeed on French soil.

The following year, the IOC met in Prague, Czechoslovakia, to learn what they could from the good and bad parts of the 1924 Games. Because the baron was retiring, they also had to choose a new president. Many of the IOC members planned not to vote for anyone, hoping the 61-year-old Coubertin could be persuaded to continue in the job. But the baron insisted on leaving.

Pierre and Marie in
Prague, 1925

The IOC member from Belgium, Count Henri de Baillet-Latour, was elected president. He had worked hard on the 1920 Games. He brought South American countries into the Games, and he had good relationships with the various International Federations.

Though the IOC couldn't convince Coubertin to stay in office, they voted him an honorary title: "President for Life of the Olympic Games." They declared that this title would never be given to any other IOC member. The baron was proud of the title, and often corrected people who thought he was "IOC President for Life."

After he retired, Coubertin continued to follow the IOC's activities. He knew that amateurism was still a matter of debate. IOC members kept making up new rules about who was an amateur. Then they would change or cancel them.

The IOC is still doing that.

13

"THE UNION OF MUSCLE AND THOUGHT"

Pierre's idea that an athlete had to be a gentleman was old-fashioned by 1904; people realized that performance was what mattered. The baron may not have liked the idea, but he had the good sense to accept it.

Another idea that the baron began to accept was that women were going to play sports and that they perhaps deserved some attention. Two months before he died in 1937, Pierre finally conceded, "Let women participate in sports if they wish, but let them not exhibit themselves doing so."[51]

During the 1928 Amsterdam Olympics the baron was too ill to attend, but he sent a message. Since he knew a trip to the 1932 Games in Los Angeles would be beyond his pocketbook, his Amsterdam message sounded like a final farewell.

> Keep ever alive the flame of the revived Olympic spirit and maintain its necessary principles....The great point is that, every-

Opposite page: The baron must have been heartened by the friendship forged between German long jumper Luz Long, left, and American track-and-field star Jesse Owens at the 1936 Games. In a fine display of sportsmanship, Long gave Owens some timely advice that enabled him to advance to the finals in the long jump.

where everyone from adolescent to adult, should cultivate and spread the true sporting spirit of spontaneous loyalty and chivalrous impartiality....Once again, I beg to thank those who have...helped me to fight a forty-year war, not often easy, and not always cleanly fought.[52]

Who did Coubertin have to fight against? Many publishers and journalists, looking for an exciting story, printed Olympic scandals and invented Olympic quarrels to sell newspapers. Teachers and intellectuals belittled sports and discouraged competition. Politicians tried to use the Olympics for their own purposes. Coubertin fought them all, using his pen and his voice for weapons.

And in a way, the baron had fought himself. He had a need for personal power and recognition. He also sensed that he must hide this need if he wanted the Games to succeed. So he brushed aside credit when it was offered and complained later about how he was cheated of honor.

The baron felt Europe slipping toward war again in the early 1930s. Because the 1932 Games were held in distant Los Angeles, they maintained the luster of peacetime Olympics. The baron could not attend because of the distance and the expense. But he heard the highlights, including a report on the freestyle swimming event, in which American Buster Crabbe won by a fingertip after lagging two full pool-lengths behind his competitor. Crabbe succeeded Weissmuller as Tarzan in the movies and went on to play Flash Gordon and Buck Rogers.

The 1936 Games, both winter and summer, were scheduled for Germany, where the Nazis were in power. Aware that the Games were to be organized by a warlike host, Coubertin again had to face the fact that international sporting competition had not led to world peace. The German leader, Adolf Hitler, made ugly, racist predictions. He claimed that blond, fair-skinned German athletes were naturally superior to all others and would win most of the events at the Games.

The Olympic Torch Relay

In recent history, the torch relay has been an integral part of the pre-Olympic preparations and the opening ceremony for both the summer and winter Games.

The only mention of the rite appears in Rule 63 of the Olympic Charter. It says, "A symbolic release of

pigeons precedes the arrival of the Olympic Flame brought from Olympia by a relay of runners, the last of whom, after circling the track, shall light the sacred Olympic fire which shall not be extinguished until the close of the Olympic Games."

In ancient days, torches, flames, and smoke were often part of religious rituals. Before each ancient Olympics, a sacred truce was declared. The beginning of the truce was announced by runners carrying torches.

The first torch relay in modern times was part of the 1936 Games in Berlin. A torch was lit in Olympia, Greece. There were ceremonies that imitated ancient rites. Then, a cone-shaped mirror caught and focused the rays of the sun. Greek runner Konstantin Kondyllis held the torch in the beam of light until some tinder, arranged around two wicks of the torch, caught fire. Kondyllis began to run, and the flame was passed from torch to torch, from runner to runner.

As runners carried the flame from Greece to Germany, each was allowed to keep his torch as a souvenir.

Nearly two weeks and 3,075 kilometers later, in the Berlin stadium, an athlete named Schilgen had the honor of lighting the huge torch that would burn for the duration of the Games.

Torch relays were featured only in the Summer Games until 1952. But for the Oslo Winter Olympics, skiers brought a flame from the home of Sondre Nordheim, a 19th-century skier known as "the god of skiing." The 1960 flame came to Squaw Valley from the same source, but since then, Olympia has been the source of fire for both winter and summer Games.

He was wrong; most of the winners were non-Germans. The big hero of the 1936 Games was an African American, Jesse Owens.

Coubertin, ill again during the summer Olympics of 1936, sent a special request for the opening ceremonies. Could musicians perform "Ode to Joy," the last movement of Beethoven's Ninth Symphony? They could—and did.

The opening ceremony of these Olympics included, for the first time, the ritual of the Olympic torch. It took 12 days to run the flame from Olympia to Berlin, and 3,075 runners took part, each running one kilometer. The baron sent the runners a message, asking that they remember that the modern Olympics were to be, above all else, educational. Wars and conflicts would never be avoided unless education discouraged such horrors, and the Games were intended to teach sportsmanship, conflict resolution, and the value of cooperation. He asked that "the union of muscle and thought may be finally sealed for the sake of progress and human dignity."[53]

Now at the fringes of the movement he created, Coubertin continued to busy himself with details of Olympic affairs. He had no real power at the IOC any more, but he continued to write letters and articles, as if to persuade himself that he was still an important part of the enterprise.

His personal life was no happier in retirement. Neither of his children, now adults, could lead an independent life. His wife was more bitter than ever and constantly reproached Pierre for her misery and poverty. Pierre privately called her "the Cat." He may have taken a room in Geneva, a short way from Lausanne, to have some peace.

While omens of war troubled Europe, the baron was nominated for the Nobel Peace Prize. He was thrilled and excited at the prospect of such a high honor; it would have crowned his career and validated his ideals about sport and peace. Unfortunately, the Nobel Committee in Norway was not inclined to choose him, mainly because his sponsor for the prize was Adolf Hitler. Hitler was not so much for Coubertin as he was against the other

Jesse Owens at the 1936 Games

nominee, Carl von Ossietzky, a pacifist and writer who was being tortured in a Nazi prison camp when he was nominated. The news that the Nobel Committee had awarded the prize to Ossietzky saddened Coubertin. Losing the prize was one more entry in his long catalogue of disappointments.

In May of the following year, 1937, the baron went for a walk in a Geneva park. He sat down on a park bench and died. He was 74 years old. The doctors said his death was probably the result of a stroke.

Baron Pierre de Fredy de Coubertin was buried in the Bois de Vaux cemetery in Lausanne—but his heart was sent to Olympia in Greece, to be buried on the grounds of the ancient Games. Over his heart's final resting place is a monument. This message is inscribed on it, in French and Greek:

A monument marks the spot in Olympia where Coubertin's heart is buried.

On June 23, the re-establishment of the International Olympic Games was proclaimed through the initiative of Pierre de Coubertin. Consequently the first modern Olympics were gloriously celebrated in the restored stadium at Athens in April, 1896, for all the people of the world, in the reign of His Majesty George I, King of Greece.

14

A Lasting Monument

Baron Pierre de Coubertin left the Olympic Games as his legacy to the world. But like any successful enterprise, the Games have a life of their own and have produced many offshoots. The most obvious of these is the International Olympic Committee.

The headquarters for the IOC is still in Lausanne, Switzerland, at Olympic House. This is a modern building on the grounds of the Château de Vidy, which is used by the IOC president and his personal staff.

At Olympic House, about 80 people from at least 10 different countries make up the Secretariat—the administration of the IOC. These people work in one or more of about 20 different departments. For instance, they might work on the Eligibility Commission, making policies about who qualifies for competition, examining credentials, and settling disputes.

Another interesting department is the Medical Commission. During the late 20th century, a lot has been learned about how to keep athletes healthy and uninjured and about how to heal them quickly

Opposite page: The IOC headquarters in Lausanne, Switzerland

without undermining their basic strength. The commission has been important in these discoveries. Also, this commission monitors the inappropriate use of drugs by athletes and explores ways to detect the use of these drugs.

One department of the Secretariat deals exclusively with worldwide postal services that want to use the Olympic rings on stamps. A license fee is charged to any postal service that wants to use the symbol. Pierre de Coubertin's picture also appears on many stamps of the world, both with and without the Olympic rings.

Licensing the Olympic symbol is only a small source of funds for the IOC. Most of its money comes from fees the IOC charges the media for the right to record the Games or to broadcast them on radio or television. Of this money collected from the media, 20 percent is given to the Olympic Organizing Committee of the current Olympiad to help set up communication systems for the press. Of the remaining 80 percent, two-thirds is for the OOC to use in presenting the Olympics and one-third is for the IOC's operating budget (to cover such basic expenses as paying the IOC's employees). The IOC

Visitors to Lausanne can see a vast amount of memorabilia in the huge Olympic Museum.

sometimes also contributes to National Organizing Committees or to International Federations.

The IOC keeps a museum of Olympic history in Lausanne. Opened in the early 1990s, it is the third museum of its kind in Lausanne. Pierre de Coubertin himself organized the first, which closed in 1970. Ten years later, His Excellency Juan Antonio Samaranch, IOC president, set up a temporary museum: one large room with dividers used as bulletin boards—one for each Olympiad.

But a visitor to the new, white-marble museum in Lausanne can see something much more impressive, an amazing variety of Olympics-related exhibits. Some trace the history of the Games, others the histories of individual sports. There are exhibits of medals, posters, and pins. For scholars doing research into the Olympic movement, there is a library containing valuable letters and other Olympic documents.

The original Olympic Cup, donated by Pierre de Coubertin in 1906, is on display at the IOC Museum. This trophy, made of gold and silver, looks like a plate on a pedestal. Another pedestal in the center of the plate supports a winged figure. A copy of the cup is awarded yearly to some large organization that has been "active in the service of sport" and has "contributed substantially to the development of the Olympic Movement."[54]

The original Olympic Cup

Another important branch of the IOC is the Court of Arbitration for Sport. If problems arise that aren't clearly settled by the Olympic rules, whether they have to do with the performance of sport or the administration or finance of sport, the court is there to rule on them quickly and with authority.

The IOC routinely wrestles with questions that bothered the baron and his contemporaries. Who is an amateur? What is an "Olympic" sport? How can judging be more impartial? How can politics be separated from international Games?

The Committee also has to deal with problems Coubertin never dreamed of. Terrorism, boycotts, commercialism, and drugs are regular topics of discussion, and new solutions to these problems are

regularly needed. Ironically, by becoming successful and influential, the Olympics—which the baron had envisioned as an instrument of peace and understanding—have sometimes become the cause of international discontent and rancor.

Not all IOC activity is located in Lausanne. The committee also developed an academy on the site of ancient Olympia. This center for learning was the pet project of an IOC member from Greece, Jean Ketseas, who saw it as one more way to keep alive Coubertin's ideas of peace and cooperation through sport. Run by Greek IOC members and their staff, the academy offers classes in subjects like athletic training, sports administration, and sports medicine.

A group based in France, the International Committee for Fair Play, keeps alive another positive part of the baron's philosophy. Since 1964 this group, which has no affiliation with the IOC or the Olympics, has awarded the Pierre de Coubertin Trophy "to athletes who demonstrate the greatest nobility of spirit." Anyone, by writing to the committee, can nominate an athlete for this award.

Pierre would have sympathized with the International Committee for Fair Play, for when it announces

Above: A terrorist peeks out of the apartment where Israeli hostages were being held during the 1972 crisis in Munich, Germany. Below: The International Olympic Academy in Olympia

its winners each year—with the kind of splashy ceremony Pierre loved so well—no one seems to notice. The award, and the reasons for giving it, are rarely reported to the public.

The United States Olympic Committee maintains two training sites for athletes. One is in Lake Placid, New York, where two Winter Olympics took place. The other is in Colorado Springs, Colorado. Each site maintains facilities for different sports. Athletes train there for short periods of time—long enough to analyze their performances and learn ways to improve.

These Olympic Training Centers can be used for non-Olympic championship games and for Olympic try-outs in certain sports. They offer a sports library and an interesting free tour for the public. If you tour the Colorado Springs Olympic Training Center, you will see only one picture of Pierre de Coubertin. And you will have to look very hard to find it!

Has the world forgotten Pierre de Coubertin?

Thousands of philatelists recognize his face in their stamp collections.

Organizations give awards in his name.

Classes in sports history regularly tell his story.

And every four years, his name may creep into the sports pages of the newspapers of the world.

Whether or not people know who the baron was, his Games are his lasting monument. Anyone who sees an opening ceremony of the Games, either at a stadium or on television, knows that these are no ordinary athletic meets. When the athletes parade with the flags of their individual countries flying in the wind; when spectators cheer for athletes from other countries; when the president of the host country announces "I declare the Games of this Olympiad open," it is easy to understand Pierre de Coubertin's passion for the Games.

The Games are about athletic excellence. They are about world peace and understanding. They are about the thrill of pageantry and the drama of competition.

There is nothing else like them.

And through them lives the spirit of a French baron who saw far, spoke true, and acted firm—Pierre de Coubertin.

One of many stamps bearing Pierre de Coubertin's image

Notes

[1] This information is from research done for *The First Century Project,* a multivolume history of the modern Olympics. As the author wrote *Coubertin's Olympics,* this ambitious project was not yet published, but was planned for release prior to the 1996 Games in Atlanta, Georgia.

[2] John J. MacAloon, *This Great Symbol,* (Chicago: University of Chicago Press, 1981), p. 27.

[3] First Century Project

[4] First Century Project

[5] Pierre de Coubertin, quoted in MacAloon, p. 55.

[6] Quoted in Richard B. Mandell, *The First Modern Olympics,* (Los Angeles: University of California Press, 1976), p. 56.

[7] First Century Project

[8] Quoted in John A. Lucas, *Baron Pierre de Coubertin and the Formative years of the Modern International Olympic Movement, 1883-1896,* (doctoral dissertation at the University of Maryland, 1963), p. 85.

[9] Quoted in Bill Henry, *An Approved History of the Olympic Games,* (Los Angeles: Southern California Committee for the Olympic Games, 1981), p. 22.

[10] First Century Project

[11] William O. Johnson, Jr., *All That Glitters Is Not Gold,* (New York: G. P. Putnam's Sons, 1972), p. 67.

[12] First Century Project

[13] First Century Project

[14] Quoted in MacAloon, p. 166.

[15] First Century Project

[16] Quoted in David C. Young, *The Olympic Myth of Greek Amateur Athletics,* (Chicago:

Ares Publishers, 1984), p. 64.

[17] MacAloon, p. 170.

[18] Quoted in MacAloon, p. 171.

[19] First Century Project

[20] First Century Project

[21] First Century Project

[22] MacAloon, p. 170.

[23] First Century Project

[24] These minutes have been compiled by Wolf Lyberg, Executive Secretary General of the Swedish National Organizing Committee, dated 1988. They are available in several libraries, including the Amateur Athletic Foundation Library in Los Angeles.

[25] First Century Project

[26] First Century Project

[27] Quoted in Henry, p. 31.

[28] Quoted in MacAloon, p. 191.

[29] First Century Project

[30] First Century Project

[31] First Century Project

[32] First Century Project

[33] Pierre de Coubertin, quoted in Henry, p. 41.

[34] Quoted in MacAloon, p. 203.

[35] First Century Project

[36] First Century Project

[37] First Century Project

[38] First Century Project

[39] From a letter to the author by Geoffroy de Navacelle (great-grandnephew of Pierre de Coubertin), September 19, 1992.

[40] Quoted in Peter Andrews, "The First American Olympics," *American Heritage Magazine,* May-June, 1988, p. 45.

[41] Lord Desborough's "Manifesto to the Press," quoted in Pierre de Coubertin's Olympic memoirs, published as "The

Fourth Olympiad, London, 1908," *Olympic Review,* No. 114, April 1977, pp. 248-52.

[42] Quoted in Dick Schaap, *An Illustrated History of the Olympic Games,* (New York: Knopf, 1975), p. 104.

[43] Coubertin, "The Fourth Olympiad"

[44] Pierre de Coubertin, "Chronique du mois," *The Olympic Review,* July 1910, pp. 109-110.

[45] Mary Henson Leigh, "The Evolution of Women's Participation in the Summer Olympic Games, 1900-1948," (Ph.D. dissertation, Columbus: The Ohio State University, 1974), p. 81.

[46] Ibid., p. 85.

[47] Quoted in Leigh, op. cit., p. 22.

[48] Pierre de Coubertin, "Olympic Memoirs," *The Olympic Review,* No. 127 May 1978, p. 305.

[49] Ibid., p 89.

[50] Coubertin, op. cit., p. 305.

[51] Quoted in Leigh, op. cit., p. 24.

[52] Quoted in Lord (Maurice) Killanin and John Rodda, *The Olympic Games 1980: Moscow and Lake Placid,* (New York: Macmillan Publishing Co., 1979), p. 87.

[53] Pierre de Coubertin, "To the Runners in the Olympia-Berlin Torch Relay," *The Olympic Review,* No. 26, August 1986, p. 451.

[54] International Olympic Committee, The Olympic Movement, Lausanne: IOC, 1987, p. 41.

Sources of Information

I consulted material in several categories in order to put together the story of *Coubertin's Olympics*.

I first searched for basic biographical facts about Pierre de Coubertin, but found I had to go to histories of the Olympic Games to get this information. The best and most useful of these is *This Great Symbol: Pierre de Coubertin and the Origins of the Modern Olympic Games* by John J. MacAloon (University of Chicago Press, 1981). It has a lot of information about the world in which Coubertin grew up, as well as insights into his character and relationships. Mac-Aloon has many quotations in translation from *Pierre de Coubertin: L'Épopée olympique*, which is the best existing biography of Coubertin, written in French by Marie-Thérèse Eyquem (Calmann-Lévy, 1966).

Other histories of the Games which helped to make the story clear were *The Modern Olympic Story* by Sandor Barcs (Corvina Press, 1964); Bill Henry's *An Approved History of the Olympic Games* (Southern California Committee for the Olympic Games, 1981); John Apostle Lucas's *Baron Pierre de Coubertin and the Formative Years of the Modern Olympic Movement* (a dissertation written for the University of Maryland in 1963); and Richard Mandell's *The First Modern Olympics* (University of California Press, 1976).

I was able to read English translations of Pierre de Coubertin's own memories in copies of *The Olympic Review*, the bulletin of the International Olympic Committee. His accounts are found in issues published in 1973 and 1974.

For information on the modern and the ancient Olympics, I used John Kieran's *Story of the Olympic Games, 776 B.C. to 1972* (Lippincott, 1973).

Other special histories include *The Work of the Turner Societies*, by Ernst A. Weier (American Gymnastic Union, 1919); Mary Henson Leigh's *The Evolution of Women's Participation in the Summer Olympic Games, 1900–1948* (Ohio State University, 1974, a dissertation); and David C. Young's *The Olympic Myth of Greek Amateur Athletics* (Ares Publishers, Inc., 1984).

I was very lucky to have access to research for a history that was not yet published when I was writing this book. Dr. Gary Allison heads a team of researchers working to compile a complete history of the first 100 years of the Games, which was to be published before the Atlanta Olympics in 1996. Their work, which is called *The First Century Project*, is being done in Los Angeles, and Dr. Allison was an invaluable resource.

For stories of events at various Games, and for specific information on who won what, when, and how, the best source is David Wallechinsky's *The Complete Book of the Olympic Games* (Little, Brown and Company, 1992). This is a great resource, but it's hard to use because it lacks an index. Another good general book with some information on the Games is Lois Decker O'Neil's *The Woman's Book of World Records and Achievements* (Anchor/ Doubleday, 1979).

Once I understood that though the motives of the IOC are quite pure, the people who run it are only human, I began to enjoy exposés—books such as *All That Glitters is Not Gold: The Olympic Games*, by William O. Johnson (Putnam, 1972); Allen Guttman's *The Games Must Go On: Avery Brundage and the Olympic Movement* (Columbia University Press, 1984); *The Olympic Games in Transition*, by Jeffrey O. Seagrave and Donald Chu (Human Kinetics Books, 1988); *Five Ring Circus: Money, Power and Politics at the Olympic Games*, by Vyv Simson (Simon and Schuster, 1982); and *The Olympic Games, 1980: Moscow and Lake Placid*, by Lord Killanin and John Rodda (Macmillan, 1979).

The International Olympic Committee has published many documents about the various traditions it upholds and the various facilities it maintains. I used *The Olympic Movement* (International Olympic Committee, 1987); *The Olympic Flames: The Great Olympic Symbol*, by Conrado Durantz (IOC, 1988); and "Lausanne, 10th April, 75 Years Ago. . . A Long Friendship," an article in *The Olympic Review* (IOC, April 1990). The Committee also courteously cooperated in answering specific questions by telefax.

Index

Photo and Illustration Acknowledgments

Photographs and illustrations in this book are reproduced by permission of: © The International Olympic Committee Archives, pp. 2-3 (by Naeder), 6, 7, 8, 10 (both), 11 (by Pierre Gory), 12 (top), 17, 18, 20, 24, 26, 30, 31, 32, 34, 36, 37, 39, 42, 45, 46 (both), 52, 54, 56, 57 (by Albert Meyer), 58, 59, 60 (all), 61, 64, 67 (by Albert Meyer), 68, 69, 70 (bottom), 71, 72, 74, 79 (both, bottom photo by Sport universal illustré), 82, 84, 86, 89, 92 (both), 93, 94, 97, 98, 99 (by Naeder), 102, 104, 105 (both), 106, 110, 111, 112, 115, 116, 117, 118, 120 (by Strahm), 121, 122 (bottom), 123; Mansell Collection, p. 12; The Bettmann Archive, pp. 14, 29, 85; Amateur Athletic Foundation of Los Angeles, pp. 23, 91, 109 (both); The Chicago Public Library/Special Collections Division, p. 38; The Cleveland Museum of Art/Purchase from Mrs. Eakins for the Hinman B. Hurlbut Collection, p. 48 (painting by Thomas Eakins); Independent Picture Service, p. 70 (top); SportsChrome East/West, p. 80 (by Robert Tringali, Jr.); Minneapolis Public Library and Information Center, p. 90; and UPI/Bettmann, pp. 100, 122 (top).

Front cover illustration is copyright © 1994 by Eric Peterson. Front cover photograph of Pierre de Coubertin is reproduced by permission of the International Olympic Committee Archives, as are the back cover photographs of the 1896 100-meter dash and Jesse Owens and Luz Long. The back cover photograph of Bonnie Blair is reproduced by permission of SportsChrome East/West (by Eileen Langsley).